Approaching retirement

A Consumer Publication

Consumers' Association
publishers of **Which?**
14 Buckingham Street
London WC2N 6DS

A Consumer Publication

edited by   Edith Rudinger

published by   Consumers' Association
publishers of **Which?**

Consumer Publications
are available from
Consumers' Association
and from booksellers.
Details are given at
the end of this book.

© Consumers' Association, August 1983
amended reprint March 1984
ISBN 0 85202 259 X
and 0 340 33163 1

Printed in Great Britain by
Whitstable Litho Ltd., Whitstable, Kent

Contents

STOP PRESS

In the budget speech on 13 March 1984 the Chancellor announced the following measures, some with immediate effect:

Life insurance (see p 47, 109, 112, 113, 115)

The income tax relief on life insurance premiums has been abolished for any life insurance contracts made after 12 March 1984. Existing policies are unaffected.

Bank interest (see p 93, 94, 97/8)

From April 1984, the interest on bank deposit accounts will be paid net of tax.

Investment income (see p 114)

From April 1984, the investment income surcharge of 15 per cent is abolished.

Age allowance (see p 24, 37, 103, 114)

For the tax year 1984/5 the age allowance is going up from £2,360 to £2,490 for a single person; married age allowance from £3,755 to £3,955. The threshold above which age allowance starts to be clawed back has been raised from £7,600 to £8,100.

Foreword

Retirement is an important event; it marks a new phase in life, and is a convenient time for taking stock and making certain decisions about the future. A big change in retirement will be in the amount of free time available, probably for the first time in over forty years, to organise your daily life without the restraints of set hours and a regular working routine. This may come as a shock to someone who has not thought how to spend his or her leisure; for others, it will be a happy release and the opportunity to do what they want, when they want to. A certain amount of planning will help you to enjoy a more content retirement: if you can remain actively involved in something – new, old or different – the continuing enjoyment of interests and activities can also contribute to health and wellbeing.

However, in spite of careful planning and enthusiastic anticipation, no one can predict what it will actually be like; do not feel disappointed if at first your retirement does not seem the happy release you anticipated. The sudden change, after years of working life, can be quite dramatic, and concern about the future may underlie the feeling of freedom: concern about getting older, becoming more dependent on others, having to manage on a progressively smaller income.

Finance is a potential source of worry for many people coming up to retirement. Some may be virtually as well-off as when they were working, but many will face a fall in income straightaway (or later on, if they are on a fixed pension). At this stage, far-reaching financial decisions may have to be taken, perhaps some – such as how to invest a lump sum – for the first time.

How you decide to organise your retirement so as to make the most of your new life is, of course, entirely up to you. This book aims to help you with some of the decisions that will face you.

ILLUSTRATIONS: ANNA KOSTAL

THINKING ABOUT FINANCE

It is worth making financial plans well before you retire – five years ahead, if you can; even two ahead is better than nothing.

Try and make as detailed a forecast as possible of what your likely income will be when you stop work and what you will need to spend your money on, and how your spending pattern might change.

It is difficult to predict this, long before retirement, and particularly difficult to take account of inflation. However, you can – and should – revise your estimate regularly to keep it up to date.

income

Your income will almost certainly fall when you retire. Instead of a regular salary or wages you will receive an income from:

☆ a basic retirement pension from the state
☆ maybe a wife's pension
☆ maybe an addition to your state pension, related to what you earned while employed
☆ possibly an occupational pension from your employer, or a self-employed pension
☆ the income from any savings and investments. But remember that if you invest your money for maximum safety, its value may not keep pace with inflation; so, it is generally sensible to make a pessimistic estimate of the income from investments
☆ other sources, such as any earnings from freelance part-time jobs.

spending

If you have never done any domestic budgeting, start with jotting down what you think your current spending pattern is. Then keep a careful detailed record for a few months – ideally for a whole year – of what you really spend (preferably day by day, or week by week). This will highlight exactly how you do spend your money now, and show how much you really need to spend on:

☆ day to day items you buy regularly (food, household goods, petrol, cigarettes)
☆ regular lump sums, to pay bills which turn up regularly and at predictable intervals (the rates, mortgage, road tax, fuel bills)
☆ leisure activities (books, cinema, pub, gardening)
☆ irregular lump sums (money spent on major items such as holidays, new washing machine, redecorating the house)
☆ unforeseeable expenditure (car repairs, a leaking roof).

The advantage of knowing where the money goes is that you can see at a glance where you could economise, if necessary, and what could be cut out altogether.

Around the time you retire, there will probably be a shift in your spending pattern. Some of this change relates to simply stopping work.

For example, you will not to have to pay fares to and from work, or for lunch out (on the other hand, you may find that you will need to spend more on food if you usually have lunch at a subsidised canteen). With more time available, you may plan to spend more on certain leisure activities, such as gardening or playing bridge. Take note of this when drawing up your budget.

Also try to take into account the effect of simply growing older. In your late sixties, you may want (or will need) to spend more than you do now, for example, on heating, on labour-saving appliances, on transport. By looking several years ahead and allowing for this kind of age-related change in spending, you stand a better chance of being realistic when you work out your future budget, than if you assume you will spend your money in the same way as you did in your forties or fifties.

what you will need

Changes in your spending are likely to occur in the following areas:

Family circumstances: your children will probably have left home and may be financially completely independent by the time you retire.

Regular financial commitments: you will probably be free of your mortgage by the time you retire. Payments into a personal pension scheme should also have ended.

Lifestyle: you may want to plan your holidays differently – travel in more comfort perhaps, or spend more on trips abroad. On the other hand, you may be able to save by being able to travel during the off-season and at reduced fares.

You may want to spend more time on, say, cooking and not rely on quickly prepared but expensive convenience food or frozen meals, but you may end up spending more money on special ingredients and on gas or electricity. There will be more time for 'entertaining' – inviting friends for drinks or a meal, for instance, which is enjoyable but also costs money. (If the invitations are reciprocated, that is also enjoyable, but not money-saving.)

There will be more time for spending money on theatres, concerts, films – but you may be able to take advantage of cheaper tickets. More time for gardening may mean growing your own vegetables more successfully; the seeds cost practically nothing, but the cost of fertilizers, insecticide, weedkillers, tools, all mount up.

Clothes: as people get older, they often need to spend more on heating the house and warmer clothing. However, you may find less need to spend money on smart clothes than when you were working. Being retired does not mean that you have to go around looking dowdy, but there will be less need for formal clothing.

Extra expenses: when you are older, you may no longer be prepared to walk in the pouring rain, so you may pay out more for bus rides (but there may well be fare concessions to take advantage of). You may also want, or will need, to get paid help with the housework.

A major cost, which cannot be postponed indefinitely after retirement, is having to replace household equipment as it, too, gets old. It is well worth buying new appliances while you are still earning if anything will need to be replaced before too long – refrigerator, washing machine, cooker. This may also be a good time to think about the car.

Inflation: You can see from the figures below how much money you would need in the future for it to be worth £1,000 at today's prices, given various rates of inflation.

	How much money you would need in future for it to be worth £1,000 at 1984 prices given a yearly inflation rate of			
	3%	6%	9%	12%
at the end of 10 years	£1,344	£1,791	£2,367	£3,106
at the end of 15 years	£1,558	£2,397¹	£3,642	£5,474
at the end of 20 years	£1,806	£3,207	£5,604	£9,646

A gap between income and spending

If it looks as if you will need more money than you are going to have in retirement, the alternatives include:

☆ spending less now on inessentials, so that you can save up for retirement while you still have a regular income
☆ moving to a smaller or less expensive home
☆ finding ways of increasing your income after retirement, by reorganising your investments to give income later
☆ taking part-time work, if you can find it
☆ choosing cheaper hobbies, getting rid of the car (which will bring a small lump sum and save running costs).

car

A car is a tremendous convenience but also a major expense: insurance, vehicle licence tax, MoT test, are basic costs even if you drive only to the shopping centre once a week. To this has to be added the cost of petrol and oil, parking fees, servicing and repairs, depreciation (that is, how much less the car will be worth if and when you sell it).

If you drive less than about 4000 miles a year, it can be cheaper to hire a car rather than own one, but this does not take into account the convenience of being able to step into your own car whenever you wish. And remember that if you hire a self-drive car, it has to be collected and returned to what may be an inconvenient point. Also, you will be driving only occasionally, and then an unfamiliar car.

If you are keeping a car, think about

☆ changing to a car that uses less petrol (both mpg and octane rating)
☆ changing to a car in a low insurance group. (You may be able to reduce the insurance premium by taking what is known as an excess, that is being willing to pay part of any claim – say £50 – yourself.)
☆ learning about car maintenance and doing some of it yourself which can save on garage bills
☆ sharing some journeys and cost with a neighbour by using the car jointly or on set alternative dates (but that may lead to the end of a long friendship).

A couple who relies on a car for transport should make sure that both people can drive: it may be necessary in an emergency, and useful in everyday circumstances.

A driving licence lasts until the driver's 70th birthday. After that, it can be renewed for three years, but you have to be medically fit. After the age of 73 (or 70 if there are medical reasons), the licence can be renewed for one year at a time, if it is supported by a doctor's certificate of fitness to drive. The doctor can charge for this (the British Medical Association's recommended fee is £20): another annual motoring expense.

In a two-car family, giving up one of the two cars could save a lot of money. This makes economic sense, but be sure you think it through and talk it over first. In some cases, where a married couple sells one car, the husband continues to think of the car as his (and the wife can become a burden to her friends).

giving up the car?

Quite apart from the saving, you would no longer have to cope with the general hassle of driving, which will become more irritating as you get older. But do not do so lightly if you think that being without a car would leave you isolated.

Amongst the advantages of having a car are the sheer convenience, not having to wait for public transport in wet and draughty conditions and not having to be exposed to colds and germs when travelling in crowded public vehicles. A car is invaluable when a necessary visit to the doctor or other medical help has to be made.

Finding work
in early retirement

If you have retired early, before qualifying for the state retirement pension, you may need to supplement your income by finding some paid work. This may not be easy because you will be competing against much younger people, but some employers may prefer an older person.

Start looking as soon as you know that you will be prematurely retired. Use the old-boy network, use your connections through pub and club, church, old business contacts: if you do not tell people that you are available, they will not know, or be aware of the fact that you are looking for a job. Tell your relations, neighbours, friends, acquaintances. And, of course, go to your local jobcentre.

Use any trade or professional institutes and societies of which you may be a member; use your trade union.

Do not forget the Professional Executive Register (PER), established by the Manpower Services Commission, or the employment agencies that specialise in particular trades, industries, professions. Find out about, and approach, local self-help groups and local centres for the unemployed run by the TUC and MSC. They tend to concentrate on younger people, but may provide opportunities for someone near retirement age.

The search may be long and tedious. You are more likely to achieve success if you present yourself well, and have a carefully prepared curriculum vitae. But you may have to be willing to take a job in a new field and may need to retrain.

retraining

A reason for having to take early retirement may be that technology has outstripped your own knowledge and experience. So, for a new career or new occupation, consider retraining.

You can approach the Training Opportunity Scheme (through your local jobcentre) and see what is available for you, at your age, and whether – and on what conditions – they will take you on. One condition is that you must be willing to take up employment in the occupation for which you train, but there is no guarantee of a job.

Examine what courses are on offer at your local adult education centre or technical college; the library is a good place to look for information and announcements. While looking for retraining courses, you may come across other courses or lectures that may be useful.

co-operatives

There has lately been a revival in small co-operatives, set up by seven or more people. A co-operative is a business venture jointly owned by the people who work in it, conducted on business lines but distributing any profits amongst its members on a democratic basis.

You, too, could get together with 6 other people and start your own co-operative. An example would be a small local gardening service with two full-time gardeners, three part-time workers with book-keeping and gardening skills, and two members working on a voluntary basis.

Further information, and a publications list, can be obtained from the Co-operative Development Agency, 20 Albert Embankment, London SE1 7TJ (telephone: 01-211 4633).

possible placement agencies

Some employment agencies which specialise in placing older people include:

Executive Standby Ltd, at 310 Chester Road, Hartford, Northwich CWA 2AB and *Executive Standby (South) Ltd,* at office 51, London Wool Exchange, Brushfield Street, London E1, and *Executive Standby (West) Ltd*, at Somercourt, Homefield Road, Saltford, Bristol BS18 3EG, have a register of executives who are available to fill short-term, and long-term, consultancy vacancies.

Intex Executive (UK) Ltd, Chancery House, 53–64 Chancery Lane, London WC2A 1QU provides senior executives or managers to employers, on a short-term basis.

Success After Sixty, 40–41 Old Bond Street, London W1X 3AF is an employment agency which will introduce to employers people over 50 who are looking for part-time or full-time employment.

Buretire (UK) Ltd, run by The Employment Fellowship, Drayton House, Gordon Street, London WC1, is an employment bureau which aims to find part-time employment for retired and disabled people.

Retired Executive Action Clearing House (REACH), Victoria House, Southampton Row, London WC1B 4DH links retired executives to useful work with voluntary organisations on an expenses-only basis; it does not find paid jobs.

helping to make ends meet

Anyone not working full-time whose income is below a certain statutory minimum, with savings of less than –at present–£3000 can apply for supplementary benefit, designed to meet ordinary living expenses. Leaflet SB1, available from social security offices, gives full details and a claim form.

People getting supplementary benefit normally have their rent and rates met in full. Others on a low income may be entitled to claim housing benefit; the amount depends on the size of the family, and the amount of rent or rates payable. Application has to be made to the housing department of the local authority.

PENSIONS

For many people, the main income in retirement will be a pension: from the state and, perhaps, an occupational or a self-employed scheme.

A pension from the state

You can receive a state pension only if you have reached the official pensionable age of 65 (for men) or 60 (for women) and have retired from your regular work. You will generally count as retired if one of the following applies:

○ you do not work at all, or
○ you do not work for more than 12 hours a week, or
○ you work only occasionally, or
○ you do not normally earn more than £65 a week (this is the limit for the year from November 1983)

When you reach the age of 70 (men) or 65 (women) you can be paid your state pension even if you have not retired.

who is eligible?

In order to qualify for a state pension, you will have to have paid or been credited with enough national insurance (NI) contributions.

national insurance contributions

National Insurance contributions have to be paid by most people who have a job and earn above a certain minimum, or who are self-employed. Employers also pay contributions, on behalf of their staff. During periods of not working and receiving certain state benefits – such as sickness, invalidity, unemployment or maternity benefit – you do not pay NI contributions but are credited with them.

Since 1975, the amount an employee pays in 'class 1' contributions is a percentage of his or her total earnings up to the 'upper limit'. This limit changes from year to year; at present it is £250 a week. Anyone earning less than (at present) £34 a week does not pay; anyone earning over £250 a week does not have to pay on the amount earned above that figure.

A self-employed person pays a 'class 2' flat-rate contribution (at present £4.60 a week), which counts towards his basic pension only.

Your state pension can comprise a *basic (flat-rate) pension* plus an *earnings-related additional pension*. You might also qualify for a small *graduated pension* under an older state pension scheme.

basic pension: who qualifies

To qualify for the basic pension, you have to pass two 'contributions tests.' The first 'test' is that you must have paid or been credited with a minimum number of NI contributions in any one tax-year during your working life, namely

○ for each tax-year you worked after 5 April 1978, the minimum is what someone who earns just enough each week to have to pay any contributions at all, would have to pay in contributions for a full 52 weeks' work. So, if you pay full class 1 or 2 (or class 3, voluntary) contributions, you will be paying at least the minimum needed
○ for each tax-year you worked from 6 April 1975 to 5 April 1978, the minimum was what someone who earned just enough to pay any contributions at all in those years would pay in contributions for 50 weeks' work
○ for any time you worked before April 1975 (when NI contributions were two tier, a flat-rate and a graduated rate) the total number of flat-rate contributions you paid during that time is divided into lots of 50 and each lot (or part-lot) is treated as a tax-year's worth of contributions to count towards the total years you need.

The second 'test' is that you must have paid, or been credited with, the relevant contributions for a given number of tax years during your working life. You will need to have contributed for nearly a quarter of the years in your working life in order to get any basic pension at all.

'working life'

In order to qualify for the full basic pension, you must have the minimum NI contributions for about 90 per cent of your working life.

Working life is an official definition. It means the tax-years from the year in which you reach the age of 16 to the tax-year ending just before you reach pensionable age. So, generally, working life for a man is 49 years, and for a woman 44 years.

But any tax year since 1978 during which you were at home caring for your children and in receipt of child benefit, or caring for an elderly or sick relative and in receipt of attendance allowance (or, in some cases, in receipt of supplementary benefit), may qualify you for home responsibilities protection. Home responsibilities protection reduces the number of years' contributions you need in order to qualify for a full basic pension. But the number of years cannot be reduced to less than twenty. Also, the years between 16 and 18 if still at school are credited towards working life. However, periods spent studying, travelling or resting count as part of your working life and will appear as gaps in your NI contributions record, unless you made voluntary NI payments during those times.

Generally, voluntary contributions can only be paid within two years of the end of the tax year to which they apply and can be paid in respect of a whole year or to complete a part year in which you paid some contributions. So this is irrelevant to long-ago gaps, but may be useful for someone taking early retirement. If you want to pay 'class 3' voluntary NI contributions, contact your local social security office who should be able to tell you if you qualify. If so, you will receive a contributions card onto which you stick the NI stamps that you can buy at the post office.

If you were born before 5 July 1932, the length of your working life may be slightly different, because the current national insurance scheme started in 1948, when you would have been over 16 years old.

You can check your contributions record with your local social security office. The address is under 'Health and Social Security, Department of' in the local telephone directory. Make sure that you include your national insurance number, so that the social security office can quickly find your records. If you do not know the number, look for it on your pay slip: it has to be quoted on it.

14 Bridstone Street
London W2 4ER
23 February 1984

National Insurance No: ZB 609624C

Dear Sirs

I wish to check my record of national insurance contributions in order to assess how much state pension I will qualify for on retirement. My date of birth is 5 January 1926 and I have been in full-time employment since October 1950. Please tell me

(a) which years count as my 'working life'

(b) whether I have made enough contributions to qualify for the full basic state pension, and, if not

(c) what periods are missing, and whether I am eligible to make voluntary contributions to cover them

(d) what my pension will be when I reach 60.

I look forward to hearing from you.

Yours faithfully

Flora Redfern

basic pension: how much

The basic pension is a flat-rate pension, that is, it is not linked to your earnings. If you meet the NI contributions tests, you will get the basic pension (it is reduced if you have not made enough NI contributions).

In the year to November 1984, the full basic pension is £34.05 a week for a single person. If a husband and wife both qualify for a pension in their own right (that is, on their own contributions), they can each draw this amount. If the wife does not qualify for a pension on her own contributions, she can receive a maximum pension of £20.45 a week based on her husband's contributions (unless he does not qualify for a full rate pension, in which case she will get less than £20.45). She gets the money herself if she is over 60: it is not added as an extra to the amount the husband gets. If the wife is under 60 and so not eligible for a pension of her own, the husband can get a dependency increase to his pension, for her. The amount is the same as her pension would be, but her earnings may reduce the amount paid.

The basic pension is adjusted each November to take account of inflation. In November 1983, pensions were increased by the change in the retail price index (the official measure of inflation) over the twelve months to May 1983. This figure was 3.7 per cent.

If you have paid fewer contributions you will receive a proportionately smaller basic pension – or none at all.

how the basic pension is scaled down:

% of working life with at least the minimum contributions	approximate % of full basic pension you will get
90 or more	100
75	84
66⅔	75
50	56
33⅓	37
25	28
less than about 22% or less than 7 years' qualifying contributions	none

earnings-related additional pension

The additional pension was introduced from 6 April 1978. As long as you have been in the scheme for at least a year and paid sufficient contributions, you will qualify for some additional pension. But a person will have to be in the scheme for at least 20 years in order to qualify for the full amount, so the maximum additional pension will only be available to people retiring after 5 April 1998. If you pay full class 1 national insurance contributions, the amount you pay above the minimum in each tax-year will qualify you for some earnings-related additional pension unless you are 'contracted-out' of the state scheme.

Some employers operate pension schemes which are contracted-out of the state additional pension scheme. For a scheme to be allowed to be contracted-out, it has to provide an occupational pension at normal retirement age which is at least as good as the state earnings-related additional pension would be.

The amount of earnings-related additional pension varies from person to person and depends on

○ how many tax-years you work between 6 April 1978 and 5 April immediately before you reach pensionable age
○ your earnings in those years
○ the increase in average earnings in the economy as a whole during those years. (This is measured by the change in the index of average earnings which is published by the Department of Employment.)

The pension is worked out as follows. Income for which you have paid the relevant NI contributions is taken for each complete tax-year since 1978, up to and including the one in which you have your 64th (59th) birthday. The relevant portion of income (at present, earnings over £34 a week up to a limit of £250) is revalued in line with the growth in overall average earnings since the income was first earned up to the time of your retirement. For anyone retiring before 1998, that is who has been in the scheme for less than 20 years, all the years since 1978 are included in the revaluing; after 1998 the best 20 years' revalued income will be selected.

The weekly additional pension you get is the sum of 1/80th of each of these years' revalued earnings, divided by 52. This is fairly complicated to work out, but your local social security office should be able to tell you how much additional pension you qualify for, per week.

A simpler way to work out very roughly how much you will get is to take your current average weekly wage, subtract the lower earnings limit of £34 and ignore any income above the upper earnings limit of £250. Take 1/80th of the result and multiply by the number of years you have worked since April 1978. The result will give you a very rough idea of the amount of additional pension you will get a week (unless the change in your earnings had been significantly different from the change in the index of average earnings).

example

> Mr Sen is retiring in 1984. He currently earns the equivalent of £170 a week and has been in the new state scheme for 6 years. He works out roughly what additional pension he will get as follows:

(A) current weekly earnings	£170.00
(B) less lower earnings limit	£34.00
(C)	£136.00
(D) ignore any earnings above the upper earnings limit	not relevant
(E) 1/80th of (C)	£1.70
(F) multiply (E) by number of full years in new state scheme (5 years)	£10.20

> Mr Sen's additional pension will be roughly £10.20 a week.

You can qualify for an earnings-related additional pension even if you do not receive a basic pension. A wife receiving a basic pension on her husband's contributions can receive earnings-related additional pension earned by her own contributions.

If you are self-employed and have therefore not paid class 1 contributions for any years since April 1978, you will not qualify for the earnings-related additional pension.

graduated pension

Graduated pensions are payable under the old state scheme which ran from April 1961 to April 1975. (Employers could choose whether or not their employees were part of the graduated pension scheme.)

You qualify if you 'earned' units under the scheme. Every £9 a woman paid in contributions and every £7.50 a man contributed, earned one unit. Currently, you get 4.44p a week in pension for each unit. The amount is increased each November to take account of inflation.

You can qualify for a graduated pension even if you are not eligible for a basic state pension. A wife getting a basic pension on her husband's contributions can receive her own graduated pension.

tax

State pensions are taxable income. This does not necessarily mean that you will have to pay tax, because you can offset your tax allowance against income.

Men and women aged 64 or over before the start of the tax year (or a man whose wife is) qualify for a special age allowance in place of the usual personal allowance. (Note that even women retiring at 60 must wait until they are over 64.) During the 1983–84 tax year, the age allowance is £2,360 a year for a single person and £3,755 for a married couple. But for every 3p by which your 'total income' exceeds £7,600 a year, you lose 2p of the age allowance. Irrespective of how high your income, the allowance will not fall below the normal personal allowances of £1,785 for a single person and £2,795 for a married couple.

'Total income' is normally your gross income less

○ interest payments you make which qualify for tax relief (for instance, on a loan for home improvements)
○ any personal pension payments you may be making
○ the gross amount of covenanted payments and any enforceable maintenance payments you make.

A Christmas bonus of (at present) £10 is paid in December to everybody receiving a retirement pension. The bonus is not taxable.

working during retirement: the 'earnings rule'

If you count as retired, you can earn up to £65 a week without losing your state pension. But for every 10p you earn over £65 and up to £69, you lose 5p of your basic pension. If you earn £69 a week or more, you lose 5p of pension for each additional 5p you earn. The additional and graduated pensions are not affected by this earnings rule.

The earnings rule applies to a wife receiving a pension based on her husband's contributions. If she earns more than £45 a week, she will lose some or all of her basic pension. The earnings rule does not apply to a man over 70, a woman over 65.

If you earn over £65 a week, and certainly if you earn £69 a week or more, you should consider postponing or cancelling your retirement and earning an increased future pension.

putting off retirement

If you decide not to retire at 65 (man) or 60 (woman), you can defer taking any state pension for up to five years. For every six days (excluding sundays) you postpone retiring, the total pension (basic, earnings-related and graduated) you eventually receive will be increased by one-seventh of a penny for every £1 of the pension you qualify for (1p for every 7 weeks of postponement). This works out at approximately $7\frac{1}{2}$ per cent for each year you put off retirement.

You will have to put off retirement for at least 7 weeks in order to start earning any increase. If you work an extra six months, the weekly pension would be about £35.31 instead of £34.05. If you work for two years, it would be about £39.11. You cannot earn any increase in respect of periods when you are receiving a state benefit, such as sickness or unemployment benefit. You do not have to pay any NI contributions if you are over pensionable age and are working – although your employer will. You have to get, and complete, form CF384 (from any social security office) to get a certificate of age exception for your employer.

If you have already retired, you can cancel your retirement and increase your eventual pension as described above. You can only cancel retirement once and it will only earn you an increased pension if you are below the age of 70 (men) or 65 (women).

If a wife is over 60 and receiving a pension on her husband's contributions, she must agree (by signing her consent on form BR432) to him cancelling his retirement and she will eventually receive a pension increased by the same percentage as his own. She can earn increments on this pension even if she is over 65.

the position of wives

A woman who pays full class 1, or class 2, or class 3, NI contributions, may qualify for a basic (and with sufficient class 1 contributions, an earnings-related) pension in her own right, based on her contribution record. If there have been breaks in her employment – perhaps while bringing up a family – she may qualify for a reduced pension.

As a general rule, if she has paid only the lower class 1 contributions, or is self-employed but paying no class 2 contributions (which is only possible for someone married on or before 5 April 1977 and who had chosen to pay lower or no contributions), she can qualify only for a basic pension based on her husband's contributions. She cannot receive this pension until her husband has reached 65 and has retired and she is 60 or over.

A woman who qualifies for a reduced pension in her own right, can claim it at 60, and then claim an increased pension based on her husband's contributions when he retires or reaches 70. This is worth doing if her own pension is lower than the amount that can be claimed on the husband's contributions – at present £20.45 a week. If she also qualifies for her own earnings-related additional pension, she can continue to receive this, even if she claims her basic pension on the husband's contributions.

If she is divorced or separated from her husband, she may be able to claim a pension on his contributions as long as she has not married again. If during any tax years up to the year of the divorce she does not meet the contribution condition for a basic pension, she may be able, in effect, to treat her former husband's contributions as her own to fill the gaps in her contributions record. Even where a divorced couple have lost all contact with each other, the DHSS (through your local social security office) should be able to trace the relevant contributions records.

the position of widows

If a woman who is already receiving a widow's pension retires at 60, it will be replaced by a basic retirement pension of at least the same amount. If she does not retire at 60, she can continue to receive the widow's pension until she is 65. She can earn as much as she likes without losing any of the widow's pension. If she marries again, she loses the widow's pension and the right to a retirement pension based on her late husband's contributions, but not any retirement pension she qualifies for in her own right.

If she works during retirement, under the earning rule she will lose some basic pension if her earnings exceed £65 a week. But if she would be eligible for a widow's pension instead of a retirement pension, the basic pension will not be reduced below the amount of widow's pension she could have got. Provided the contribution conditions are satisfied, a widow may draw her retirement pension at age 60. Her late husband's age is irrelevant.

A woman over 60 whose husband dies before receiving a state retirement pension will qualify for the pension her husband would have received if he had already been retired.

A woman who is over the age of 60 when she is widowed and whose husband, but not she, was in receipt of a retirement pension at the time of his death, qualifies for a retirement pension, without needing to retire from employment.

When she retires, she will receive the single person's basic pension of up to £34.05. The amount she receives will be based on her own contributions or her late husband's – possibly both. She will be entitled to her own graduated pension and half her husband's. She will also qualify for any additional pension earned by her own or her late husband's additional contributions, subject to the maximum a single person can get. She will also get any increases in pension earned by her or her husband deferring retirement.

A man who is widowed after 6 April 1979 and could receive a higher pension by claiming on his wife's contributions, may be able to do so.

how to claim your pension

About four months before your 65th (man) or 60th (woman) birthday, your local social security office should send you the appropriate claim form.

If you have not received it by the time you are three months from your birthday, you should write to the social security office nearest to your home, saying that you will reach the age of sixty-five (sixty) on such-and-such a date and would be grateful if you could be sent the appropriate form.

If you are deferring your retirement, you must nevertheless fill in and return the form. Then, when you intend to retire you should notify the local social security office approximately four months ahead of time that you want to start claiming your state retirement pension. If you do not know in advance, let them know as soon as possible because your pension will not usually be backdated for more than three months after you have retired.

how the pension is paid

The pension can be paid once a week, in advance, through a post office. You have to specify at which office. Most pensions are paid on thursdays, so it may be worth arranging with your employer to retire on a wednesday. This does not mean that you have to collect your pension every week on thursday. The individual weekly orders in the order book you receive can be cashed for up to three months from the date shown on each. Anyone unable to collect a weekly pension can appoint an agent to collect it, by completing the authorisation on the back of the weekly order.

You can also choose to have the pension paid directly into your bank account (current or deposit), or National Girobank or National Savings Bank investment account or an investment account with most building societies. When the pension is paid directly into an account, it will be paid four-weekly or quarterly in arrears. If you decide to receive your pension in this way, ask for form NI105 (which contains an application form) at any local social security office.

It is up to you to notify the local social security office if you earn more than £65 in any one week. The adjustment to your pension is made retrospectively (possibly not till the following tax year, if your pension is paid direct into your account).

If you have to go into hospital, you can continue to receive your usual pension for the first eight weeks you are in hospital. But after that, your pension is usually reduced by £13.10 a week if you are single, or £6.55 if you have dependants.

If you intend to live, or holiday, abroad for less than three months, you can collect all the pension for that period on your return. If you will be out of the country for longer, you may be able to arrange for your pension to be paid abroad or into a UK bank. Alternatively, you can authorise someone to collect your pension on your behalf.

Leaflet NI38, available from social security offices gives details of how going abroad affects your retirement pension.

information leaflets

The Department of Health and Social Security has issued a number of explanatory leaflets and booklets available from social security offices and citizens advice bureaux. They are updated and changed at irregular intervals. The current ones include:

N127A/Feb 84 NI contributions for 1983/84 – People with small earnings from self-employment;

NI42/Oct 82 National Insurance Voluntary Contributions

NI48/July 82 National Insurance – Unpaid and late paid contributions

NI92/Nov 80 Earning extra pension by cancelling your retirement

NI105/Oct 82 Retirement pensions and widows' benefits Payment direct into banks or building societies

NI177A/Oct 82 Was your husband over 65 in 1948?

NI184/Oct 82 Non-contributory Retirement pension for people over 80

NI196/Nov 83 Benefit rates

NI208/Apr 84 National Insurance Contribution rates

NP27/Feb 80 Looking after someone at home?

NP32/Oct 82 Your retirement pension

NP32A/Nov 80 Your retirement pension if you are widowed or divorced

NP32B/Nov 81 Retirement benefits for married women

NP36/Mar 82 Your benefit as a widow after the first 26 weeks.

FB2/Nov 83 Which benefit?

A pension from your job

Many employers run their own pension scheme to provide, in addition to the state basic pension, what is known as an 'occupational' pension for their employees when they retire. There are two categories of occupational pension: not contracted-out are those schemes whose members also make full national insurance contributions, and who are eligible for the basic state pension plus additional earnings-related pension; contracted-out are those whose members pay lower national insurance contributions, and are eligible for the basic state pension only.

About half this country's workforce belong to a pension scheme run by their employer. These schemes are a form of saving; the money that is invested is used to finance members' pensions after retirement. Such schemes benefit from significant tax concessions, and the employer contributes towards your pension, too.

The return on invested contributions is free of all income and capital gains tax, so the money grows more in a pension scheme than in most other savings schemes.

contributory and non-contributory schemes

In a 'contributory' scheme, you yourself pay regular contributions into the pension scheme. The contributions are usually a fixed percentage of your salary or basic wage, say 5 per cent. Contributions of up to 15 per cent of salary can be paid out of income before tax, so are free of tax at your highest rate. For example, if you pay tax at a highest rate of 50 per cent, each £100 you contribute costs you only £50 out of your net pay.

Your employer pays the balance of the cost of providing members' pensions. The amount he contributes is also free of tax.

Some schemes are 'non-contributory', in which case you pay no contributions at all and your employer meets the full cost of the pension scheme. (But you might be paying something towards it indirectly: perhaps through lower wages; or the benefits offered under the scheme may be less generous than if the scheme were contributory.)

The contributions from employees and employer are invested to provide the funds for a company pension scheme. There are two main ways of organising a company pension scheme (the employee cannot choose which is offered).

The contributions may be paid into a pension fund run by a group of trustees. The trustees may comprise members of the company's management and staff. They administer the fund, deciding on how the money is invested – in Government stock, shares, property and so on – and they are responsible for making sure that the benefits the scheme offers (which may be not only retirement pension, but also widow's pension, and life assurance) are paid as appropriate in accordance with the rules of the trust. Alternatively, the contributions may be paid over to an insurance company which invests them and pays the benefits as they fall due.

earlier retirement age

Company pension schemes do not have to stick to the state retirement age, although many do take a standard age of 65 for men and 60 for women.

non-voluntary

If you retire early through ill-health, your pension can be worked out in a number of ways:

○ a fraction (1/80th or 1/60th) of the final pay you are earning at the time you retire for each year you would have worked if you had stayed on to normal retirement age. For example, Jim Harris retires at 55 after 15 years with his firm. He earns £8,000 when he retires and, but for ill-health, would have worked on until 65. His company pays him 1/60th of his final pay for each year he would have worked if he had stayed until he was 65 – that is, 25 years. So Jim gets a yearly pension of $25 \times \dfrac{(£8,000)}{60} = £3,333$

○ as above, but based only on the years you have actually worked. If in the above example Jim got a pension of 1/60th of final pay but only for each year he had worked, his pension would be $15 \times \dfrac{(£8,000)}{60}$ – that is a yearly pension of £2,000.

o the pension may be reduced further because it starts earlier and is therefore expected to be paid for longer.

voluntary

If you retire early voluntarily or because you are made redundant, you may be able to get a pension straightaway if you are at least 50. The age depends on the rules of the particular scheme, and may be younger if the normal retirement age in your occupation is earlier (for example, the normal retirement age for professional footballers is 35).

Your pension may be worked out in the second of the ways outlined above. This reduces the pension to substantially less than you would have got by staying on because it is based on fewer years' membership and on lower final pay.

The more usual practice, however, is that another factor is applied, reducing the pension still further, because you are likely to be getting it for more years than originally anticipated. The pension may be reduced by, say, half a per cent for each month before 'normal retirement date' of the scheme.

If you are thinking of retiring early, make sure that you are fully aware of the way your firm's pension scheme deals with this, and the basis on which your pension will be calculated, so that you know the facts and figures before you make your decision and at a time when you can still do something about the pension.

Even retiring just five years early could reduce the pension you get by one-third.

Inland Revenue rules

The government puts various restrictions on the amount you can invest and the benefits you can receive. The rules are complex, but the most important ones are that

o an employee's contributions must not exceed 15 per cent of taxable income (which includes taxable value of benefits other than pay)
o the maximum pension is $\frac{2}{3}$ of final pay on retirement at pension age 60 after at least 10 years' membership of the scheme.

Pension age has to be defined in advance; it may be as low as 60. If, however, the normal pension age under a scheme is fixed at age 65 and a member subsequently retires at age 60, the Inland Revenue may insist on the pension being reduced to take into account early retirement factors, and may not approve payment of the full two-thirds of final pay.

○ part of the pension may be taken as tax-free lump-sum instead, but it must not exceed 1½ times the final pay after at least 20 years' membership.

contracted-out schemes

If the scheme you belong to is contracted-out, your employer has taken over from the state the responsibility for paying you the earnings-related additional pension. He must pay you at least the amount you would have received from the state – that is 1/80th of your revalued earnings for each year of membership up to a maximum of 20 years. This part of your pension is called the guaranteed minimum pension (or GMP). In fact, your pension from employment is likely to be greater than the GMP.

The GMP is revalued in line with the index of average earnings; it is index-linked until the time you retire – even if you change jobs and take a preserved pension from your previous employer. Once you retire, your employer pays you a fixed GMP, but the state pays you the extra needed to increase it in line with inflation. This is normally paid together with your basic state retirement pension.

preserved pensions

You may have left a pension scheme, in the past, when you changed your job. If you chose to take a preserved (also called frozen or deferred) pension, the scheme you left will pay you a pension when you retire. The amount is usually fixed at the time you left the scheme. Some schemes allow the preserved pension to increase – usually by a fairly modest amount, say 3 per cent a year – in the years between your leaving the scheme and retiring. The government is considering a change in the law, so that preserved pensions will have to be increased in line with inflation or by 5 per cent a year, whichever is lower.

If the scheme you left was contracted-out of the state pension scheme, it must provide you with a deferred pension at least equal to the amount you would have received under the state scheme (the guaranteed minimum pension). This element of your deferred pension will be index-linked in the years between your changing jobs and retiring.

If you are entitled to a preserved pension from a previous employer, keep any explanatory booklet about the scheme and ask the trustees to give you a letter explaining your entitlement to a pension and any other benefits (and keep it safe, perhaps with your will).

It is important to let the trustees know if you change your address and it is worth getting in touch with the scheme once every five years or so, to find out if there have been any changes in the scheme's rules which will affect your entitlement.

how much pension?

The pension you get may be worked out in one of several ways. Most common are final pay schemes.

final pay scheme

The pension, including GMP if the scheme is contracted out, depends on

o the number of years you have been a member of the scheme
o your earnings at the time you retire.

Your pension might work out as 1/80th of final pay for each year you have been in the scheme. Most schemes take 40 years as the maximum service. So, after 40 years or more, you would get a pension of one-half your final pay. A more generous scheme might give you 1/60th of final pay for each year of service – so, after 40 years you would get the maximum pension allowed by the Inland Revenue, which is two-thirds of final pay.

Definitions of final pay vary, it may mean

○ the average of the best three consecutive years' pay in the last thirteen years, OR
○ basic salary in the last year plus average overtime pay, commission and bonuses during the last three years, OR
○ average yearly pay during the last few years – say three or five.

In a final pay scheme, the pension you will receive is automatically increased, with your earnings, up to the time you leave your job.

example

> Dorothy Michaels has been with her present firm for thirty years. She is now earning £18,600. When she retires shortly at the age of 60 she will get a pension equal to 1/60th of final pay for each year of service. Dorothy works that out as £310 for each of the thirty years which gives her a pension of £9,300 per annum.
>
> Before she joined her present firm, she worked ten years for another. They also had a final pay pension scheme. When Dorothy left that firm, she was earning £700 a year. The scheme pays 1/80th of final pay for each year of service, thus Dorothy gets £8.75 for each of the ten years making £87.50 a year.
>
> So Dorothy's total pension from her lifetime employment is £9,300 plus £87.50 making £9,387.50 a year in all.
>
> If her 'final pay' had been defined as the average over the last five years, this is what would be taken into consideration:
>
> She had been earning £18,600 for six months, and before that £17,500 for twelve months, £16,500 for twelve months, and £15,400 for two-and-a-half years. Her 'final pay' was £16,360 and her pension £8,180 per annum plus the £87.50 from the previous job, making a total of £8,267.50 in all.

So if your scheme is a final pay one, make sure you know how your 'final pay' will be calculated.

average pay schemes

The pension is based on the pay you received each year you were in the scheme. This is likely to result in a smaller pension than under a final pay scheme because levels of pay in the early years drag the average well below the level earned just before retirement.

example

> On retirement, Hamish Gray will get a preserved pension from a previous employer. He worked for that firm for ten years and the pension worked out as a fixed amount for each year his earnings were within a specified band. The bands were:
>
> | | |
> |---|---|
> | up to £2,999 a year | £40 |
> | £3,000 a year up to £3,999 | £50 |
> | £3,999 a year and over | £60 |
>
> Hamish's earnings work out at three years each in the first two bands and four years in the last band, so his preserved pension works out as
>
> | | |
> |---|---|
> | 3 × £40 | = £120 |
> | 3 × £50 | = £150 |
> | 4 × £60 | = £240 |
>
> total pension = £510 per annum.

Not many pension schemes, nowadays, are average pay schemes.

flat rate schemes

You are paid a fixed amount of pension, say £10 a year, for each year you were a member of the scheme.

example

> Jill Banker has been a member of her firm's pension scheme for the last 10 years. When she retires shortly she will get a pension equal to £10 for each year of service which works out at a pension of £100 a year.

Very few pension schemes, nowadays, are flat rate ones.

money purchase schemes

In this type of scheme, your own and also your employer's contributions are a fixed proportion of your earnings. They are invested and, when you retire, the accumulated sum is used to buy an immediate annuity. So the pension you get depends on

o the amount of contributions
o the rate of return on the invested contributions
o the length of time they are invested
o annuity rates at the time you retire.

Because some of these factors are unpredictable, it is not possible to calculate in advance what your pension will amount to under a money purchase scheme.

effect of state pension

Some schemes make a deduction from either final pay or the pension itself to make allowance for the pension you will get from the state. A common deduction is 1/40th of the basic state pension for each year you were in the pension scheme.

tax

A pension from your job is taxed in the same way as earnings; you get it after tax has been deducted. If the pension together with other income amounts to more than £7,600, it will effect the age allowance.

tax-free lump sum

Some pension schemes offer a lump sum on retirement as part of the deal. With most others, you can choose to exchange part of your pension for a lump sum paid on retirement. The lump sum is tax-free, but the Inland Revenue limits the amount to a maximum of 1½ times final pay after 20 or more years' service. A man retiring at age 65 can expect a lump sum of around £9 for each £1 of pension he forgoes; a woman retiring at 60 can expect about £11 for each £1 she forgoes (women get more because their pension is expected to be paid for longer).

If your pension is inflation-proofed, this is so valuable that you should be wary of exchanging any of it for a lump sum. But if you do not expect worthwhile increases in your pension during retirement, it could pay you to exchange as much as possible and invest the lump sum.

In theory, all occupational pensions could be inflation-proofed, in practice, only some are. For instance, for people employed by the government or elsewhere in the public sector, the pension during retirement will be index-linked to changes in the retail price index.

Your own pension may be increased, perhaps annually or at the discretion of your former employer. The maximum increase allowed by the Inland Revenue is the increase in the RPI.

other benefits

Your company's scheme may offer some or all of the following benefits, so make sure that you know what you may be entitled to.

life assurance cover

A lump sum is paid if you die before retirement; the Inland Revenue restricts this benefit to a maximum of four times your yearly pay (plus the contributions made and interest earned on them). Technically, the trustees decide who will receive the benefit since this avoids capital transfer tax; but in practice, they will usually pay it to anyone you nominate.

If you die after retirement, there is usually no life assurance benefit. But some schemes guarantee to pay your pension for say, five years after retirement. If you die during this period, the balance of the five years' pension may be paid as a lump sum to your dependants.

widow's/widower's pension

If a man dies before retirement, the maximum pension the widow can get under Inland Revenue rules is $\frac{2}{3}$ of the retirement pension he would have got based on earnings to date. So, if you would have qualified for a pension of £3,000, the maximum pension your widow could get is $\frac{2}{3}$ of £3,000 – ie £2,000 a year.

Usually, the widow's pension is $\frac{1}{2}$ of what the man's pension would have been. Sometimes this benefit is automatically available to all members of the pension scheme. Alternatively, it might only be available to those who have paid extra contributions. Some schemes do not offer a widow's pension at all.

Usually the widow's pension is increased by the same amount as the husband's retirement pension would have been. The widow's pension may stop if the widow remarries.

If you die during retirement, the maximum widow's pension allowed under Inland Revenue regulations is $\frac{2}{3}$ of the pension you were receiving – most schemes pay $\frac{1}{2}$. Often, you will have to decide, at the time you retire, whether or not you want to provide this benefit. If so, you may have to accept a lower retirement pension.

Widower's pensions calculated in the same way as widows' pensions are allowed by the Inland Revenue, but are not common.

know the facts

You should talk to your company's pensions manager, pension fund trustee or trade union representative to find out how your own scheme works, and what pension you will get. You may be able to increase your pension by making additional voluntary contributions.

additional voluntary contributions (AVCs)

By the time you retire, your pension income will already be determined for the most part. So if you're in your 50's, say, it is a good time to check what pensions you will get and to make arrangements to enhance your retirement income, if necessary.

With many schemes you can, if you wish, make extra contributions to your employer's pension scheme. Your regular contributions plus any voluntary ones must not exceed 15 per cent of your taxable pay. The AVCs will normally buy extra years' membership of your scheme, or a fixed addition to your pension on retirement. If the scheme is flexible enough, the fund accumulated through AVCs can be used for any benefit so long as it does not exceed the Inland Revenue limits, for instance a tax-free lump sum, extra years, a pension for dependants, inflation proofing, a guaranteed life of pension even if you die. The rules of the scheme may well be more flexible than the individual employee is led to believe, so it is worth finding out exactly what you can get.

You should look on AVCs as a method of saving – they have the advantage of full tax relief on contributions. They can be a good way of enhancing your pension if you are approaching retirement but have not been a member of your pension scheme for long enough to qualify for the full benefits. This may be particularly useful for a married woman who has not been working continuously for enough years.

sources of information

When you joined your pension scheme, you were given an explanatory booklet which should explain the scheme. If it does not answer your specific queries, take any questions or problems you have to your employer's pension manager, the trustees of the pension fund or your trade union.

There are several organisations which publish information on various aspects of occupational pensions. These include

Company Pensions Information Centre, 7 Old Park Lane, London W1Y 3LJ.

Occupational Pensions Board, Lynwood Road, Thames Ditton, Surrey KT7 0PP.

The Trade Union Congress, Congress House, Great Russell Street, London WC1 3LS.

In addition, your local social security office will have several leaflets giving information relating to company pension schemes. Your local branch of Age Concern may be able to help. The information department of Age Concern England is at Bernard Sunley House, 60 Pitcairn Road, Mitcham, Surrey CR4 3LL (telephone: 01-640 5431). Also, your local citizens advice bureau may be able to help and can put you in touch with the Occupational Pensions Advisory Service, an independent service which has been set up to advise individual members of company schemes.

Personal pension schemes

A self-employed person (that is one who pays class 2 NI contributions) is not eligible for the state earnings-related additional pension and does not have access to a pension scheme through his or her job. To fill this gap, the Inland Revenue allows special tax concessions on money they invest into an approved personal pension scheme.

You can also invest in such a scheme if you do not belong to an employer's pension scheme, either because he does not run such a scheme or because you have chosen not to join a voluntary scheme. If you belong to an employer's occupational pension scheme, you cannot also take out a personal pension relating to those earnings. You could only do so if it were related to additional earnings from a separate source.

what are they?

Personal pension schemes are pension schemes run by insurance companies for individuals; you pay premiums to the company who invests them. When you retire, the company pays you a pension until you die; part of that pension can usually be exchanged for a tax-free lump sum on retirement.

Note that once you have invested in one of these schemes, you cannot usually cash in your policy and get your money back until you retire and draw your pension.

tax advantages

A personal pension scheme is basically a savings scheme with special tax advantages, both on the premiums you pay and on some of the benefits you get. It is therefore a very efficient way of saving for retirement. You can invest a maximum of 17½ per cent (more for anyone born before 1916) of your *net relevant earnings* (roughly, your earnings in non-pensionable employment less items allowable for tax) each year in a personal pension scheme. You get tax relief on the premiums at your highest rate of tax.

The pension you get is taxed as earned income. But you can exchange part of the pension for a tax-free lump sum.

premiums

Most companies offer both regular-premium and single-premium policies. With a regular-premium policy, you agree to make regular payments, usually every month or year. The terms of your pension plan are decided when you take out the policy. Many schemes are fairly flexible and will allow you to make additional payments at any time in the future. You may also be able to vary the amount of each premium or miss some altogether – this is an important option if you are self-employed and your earnings vary from year to year.

With a single-premium policy, you pay just one lump sum. The terms of your pension plan are decided when you pay the premium. You can have more than one single-premium policy (perhaps taken out at different times). You can decide exactly how much you want to invest – although some companies will not accept single premiums smaller than £1,000.

the pension plans

The pension you get and how it is worked out will vary from company to company and depend on the type of plan. There are two main types of plan:

Deferred annuity plan: the amount of pension you will get was decided when you took out the policy. For example, if you paid £1,000 a year for 10 years from age 55, you might be quoted a pension of £1,500 a year if you retire at 65.

Cash-funded plan: the amount of pension was not set at the time you started the policy. Your premiums are invested and the accumulated fund is used to buy an immediate annuity at the time you retire, to provide your pension. So the pension you get will depend on

o the amount paid in premiums
o the return on the invested premiums
o the annuity rate at the time you retire.

For example, suppose you pay £1,000 a year from age 55. By the time you reach 65, the accumulated fund might have grown to £20,000. If annuity rates are 10 per cent at that time, your pension would be £2,000 per annum.

Normally you do not have to buy an annuity from the same company you invested with, so it is worth shopping around for the highest pension you can get at the time you retire – even if it means transferring your investment to another company.

It is useful to be able to delay retirement for a while, say for two years, if annuity rates are particularly poor, or the stock market is particularly depressed, at the time you had planned to retire.

how your premiums are invested

There are four main types of pension policy from which you can choose.

Non-profit: your premiums go into the insurance company's pension fund which the company invests as it thinks fit – mainly in shares, British Government stocks, loans and property. Irrespective of what happens to these investments, the amount of pension or cash fund you get is guaranteed by the company at the outset – it will not be more or less. You know exactly how much your pension will be. But these guaranteed pensions are low, because the company must feel certain it can pay out the agreed amounts, whatever happens to its investments and to interest rates in the meantime.

With-profits: your premiums are invested as above. The company guarantees from the outset the minimum pension it will pay you (if the policy is a deferred annuity one), or the minimum amount of money you will have for buying an annuity (if it is cash-funded). As the company makes profits on its investment, it announces increases in the minimum pension you are guaranteed at retirement. These increases are called *reversionary bonuses*, and once they have been declared (usually every year or every three years) they cannot be taken away. With most policies, a one-off *terminal bonus* may be added at the time you retire. But you will not know how much this will be until the time arrives.

Unit-linked: with this type of policy you have some choice as to how your money is invested. Your premiums buy units in one of the funds offered by the insurance company. The most common types of fund are:

○ *property funds* – which invest in office blocks, factories, shops and so on

○ *equity funds* – which invest in shares (either directly, or via unit trusts)

○ *fixed-interests funds* – which invest in securities which pay out a fixed income (eg British government stocks, company loan stocks)

○ *cash funds* – which invest in bank deposit accounts, short-term loans to local authorities and other investments which pay rates of return that vary with interest rates in general

○ *managed funds* – which invest in a mixture of the things listed above.

Each fund is divided into a number of units. The price of each unit is, approximately, the value of the investments in the fund divided by the number of units that have been issued – so the unit price goes up and down as the value of the investments in the fund fluctuates. But with cash funds, most companies guarantee that the price of units will not go down.

In general, how well you do from a unit-linked policy depends a lot on when your money goes in, and out. If the unit price was at a peak when you paid your money in, and in a trough when you draw your money out, you will not do at all well.

You can normally choose which funds to invest in and you can switch from one fund to another (for example, from the equity fund to the property fund). This could prove useful if you want to move your money around in the hope of getting the best return. But there is often a charge for switching, which may be as high as $\frac{1}{2}$ per cent of the amount you move.

Nearly all unit-linked policies are cash-funded, so the amount of pension you get will depend not only on how well the investments do, but on annuity rates at the time you start taking the benefits.

A few unit-linked policies guarantee a minimum cash fund at retirement (for example, not less than the total premiums paid), and some guarantee a minimum annuity rate – but these guarantees tend to be low.

Deposit administration: these schemes work rather like a bank deposit account. Your premiums are put into an account with the insurance company, and interest is added from time to time. The interest rate will vary, depending on the general level of interest rates – so deposit administration policies tend to look attractive in times of high interest rates. There may be a guaranteed minimum interest rate or it may, for example, be linked to The Building Societies' Association's recommended mortgate rate.

All deposit administration schemes are cash-funded, and a few of them guarantee you a minimum amount of cash fund at retirement.

choosing a policy

With a non-profit policy, you know just how much pension you will get, but the return is comparatively low. It is usually only worth considering this type of policy if you are fairly close to retirement and want to know exactly where you stand.

Deposit administration policies and the cash funds of unit-linked policies are very dependent on the level of interest rates which can vary a great deal over the long term. But the value of your fund or price of your units cannot go down, so such a policy may suit someone nearing retirement who does not want to risk losing any money.

For the long term, the choice is really between with-profits and unit-linked policies. With-profits schemes are the less risky of the two. Although the guaranteed pension or guaranteed cash fund is initially low, it is virtually certain to increase steadily over the period – once a bonus has been added to your fund, it cannot be taken back.

With unit-linked policies, the return you get depends on when you made your payments and when you start taking the benefits. These policies will tend to increase in value as prices generally rise, so there is likely to be some protection against inflation.

retirement age

You must start to take the benefits from a policy sometime between your 60th and your 75th birthdays (70th with some policies), unless your job is one that is recognised as having a lower normal retirement age. For example, pilots, female nurses and midwives can start taking benefits at 55, while boxers can start at 50. You do not need to have stopped working in order to draw your pension.

If you become too ill to work before the lowest age at which you can retire, you can start taking the benefits then. Of course, the sooner you start taking the benefits, the smaller will be the pension, because you will have been paying in and earning interest for a shorter period and are likely to be drawing out for longer. If your policy has not been going many years, taking the benefits even one year earlier will substantially reduce your pension.

With some policies, you have to say at the outset when you intend to retire (though you can change your mind later). Other policies have a standard retirement age, but do allow you to retire when you like within a given age range. If you have to say when you intend to retire, it is worth saying the earliest possible age, because you might lose out if you retire earlier than you had originally said. If you then retire later, usually your eventual pension will increase for each year you delayed retirement (and, with cash-funded policies, your fund will continue to increase).

phasing your retirement

You may not want to stop work suddenly but would rather slide out gradually over a period of years. You may want to supplement your earnings over this period by drawing a small amount of pension, increasing this year by year until you draw your full pension when you have stopped working altogether. You could do this by having several policies and taking the benefits from each at different times.

if you die before retirement

With most policies, a lump sum will be paid out to your heirs if you die before you have started getting the policy benefits. You may have a choice as to how much will be paid out – for example, return of only the premiums you have paid, or return of premiums plus interest on them.

The more you want paid out on your death, the less pension you will get. So it might be better to get the biggest pension you can and to arrange extra life insurance separately.

life insurance

In addition, or alternatively, you may wish to make provisions for your dependants by taking out a life insurance policy which pays a lump sum on your death (or one where the equivalent of a lump sum is paid to your dependants in instalments). The size of the lump sum depends on the premiums paid (which are related to your age, too: the older you are when taking out the insurance, the higher the premiums are likely to be). But there is a 15 per cent tax relief on the premiums.

If you qualify for a personal pension scheme, you also qualify for special protection-only life insurance policies (known as Section 226A policies after the section of the Taxes Act which deals with these policies). You get income tax relief on the premiums at your highest rate of tax instead of the normal premium relief of 15 per cent. To get full tax relief, the premiums must not come to more than 5 per cent of your net relevant earnings and they will count as part of the $17\frac{1}{2}$ per cent limit on premiums you can invest in a personal pension scheme.

You do not have to get Section 226A life insurance cover from the same company as the one from which you get your pension – though they may give you a discount.

widow's/widower's pension

There are two ways of providing an income for your husband or wife (or other person you name) if you die after you have started drawing the pension. The first way is to choose to have your pension paid as long as you or someone else is alive (called a *joint life and survivor annuity*). The pension may continue at the same level, or you can normally arrange for it to be higher while you are both alive. What you get would be less than a pension payable on one life only; for example a joint-life pension where both are 65 and the pension stays level after the death of the first to die, might be around 15 per cent lower.

Or you can choose to have your pension paid for a certain minimum period (often five or ten years) whether you live that long or not. This removes the risk of getting virtually nothing back if you die soon after retirement, but the pension you get at age 65 will be around 4 per cent less if it is guaranteed for five years, 10 per cent if it is guaranteed for ten years. If you live on beyond the five (or ten) years, you continue to get your pension until your death. But your dependants would be left with nothing from the plan after your death.

inflation

The buying-power of a fixed pension can be quickly eaten away by inflation. You could, instead, choose a pension which increases each year. But the pension will be smaller to start off with. For example, a pension which increases by 5 per cent compound each year will start off at about $\frac{3}{4}$ of the amount of a level pension, catching it up in six years or so. The longer you live, the better value you get from an increasing pension.

With many unit-linked policies you can choose to have your pension unit-linked, so it will go up and down in line with the price of units in the fund. This could be a good idea for part of your pension, but it would be risky to link too much of it in this way because the price of units might slump.

sources of information

If you have already invested in a personal pension scheme, the company should be able to help you with any queries. Make sure that you have, and have understood, all the information relevant to your particular scheme, and that you are aware of any choices that you may still be able to make at this stage.

brokers and consultants

You can get information and advice about these schemes from financial consultants and brokers.

The following professional bodies will supply a list of their members in a particular area:

The British Insurance Brokers' Association, 130 Fenchurch Street, London EC3M 5DJ (telephone: 01-623 9043).

The Corporation of Mortgage, Finance & Life Assurance Brokers, 6–7 Leapale Road, Guildford, Surrey GU1 4JX (telephone: 0483 39121).

The Society of Pension Consultants, Ludgate House, Ludgate Circus, London EC4A 2AB (telephone: 01-353 1688).

A consultant or broker will either be paid by commission from the insurance company you invest with, or he will charge you a fee. Make sure you know which before you seek advice. With insurance companies which do not offer commission to brokers, you would need to contact the companies direct, to find out about their pension schemes.

It is best to have some knowledge about the types of scheme on offer before you go to a consultant or broker, so get brochures on various plans from a few companies first. You may need to check with more than one consultant or advisor in order to find the best deal for you.

specialist magazines

You can also get a lot of information about different policies, current annuity rates, and so on, by looking in specialist magazines such as *Money Management* (£2.75 by post from Minister House, Arthur Street, London EC4R 9AX), *Policy Market* (£1.50 from Stone & Cox (publications) Ltd., 44 Fleet Street, London EC4Y 1BS), *Planned Savings* (£2.50) and *The Savings Market* (£5.00) (both available from Wootton Publications. 150/152 Caledonian Road, London N1 9DR).

some relevant *Which?* reports

Which? has published a number of reports covering various aspects of retirement pensions. These include:

A pension from your job, in *Money Which?* September 1976, Your pension rights when you change jobs, in *Money Which?* September 1978, Personal pension plans, in *Money Which?* December 1980, Your state retirement pension, in *Which?* October 1983.

Some of the *Money Which?* short reports include: *Which state benefit for pensioners?* in December 1982 and *Earnings rule*, in June 1981.

Most public reference libraries have copies of *Which?* magazine to which you can refer.

WHERE TO LIVE

You may have had to live in a particular area because of your work; now may be your chance to get away.

When comparing the advantages of staying in the existing home with those of moving, you should try to think objectively about where you are living at present before making a decision, and answer some questions honestly:

⋆ Do you like your present home, and its environment? This will matter more when you have to spend the greater part of the day there. Being at home all day will make you more aware of the limitations and drawbacks of your environment.

☆ Is your home large enough, light enough, warm enough, comfortable enough?

☆ Do some of your family live nearby, or a particular friend? Do you get on with your neighbours? Do you like your doctor? Are you involved in many local activities? Can you get to the shops, post office, library, club, church easily?

Shops and public transport and other facilities may be too far away when the time comes to give up the car, or inconveniently located – for instance, on the other side of a busy road, or up a steep hill.

☆ Have you got the garden just as you like it?

garden

Look particularly at the garden – is it large enough for your future gardening plans? Will it be too large to manage on your own in five, ten, twenty years' time? Can it be converted into an easy-care garden with minimal flower beds, no vegetable plots, no herbaceous border, more perennials?

Gardening involves quite hard physical work; bending and lifting get more difficult as people get older, particularly for someone suffering from arthritis.

Traditionally, gardening is high on the list of a retired person's activities, but if you dislike it or have always found it a chore, a large garden might be one factor in deciding to move.

should you move?

The main reason for considering a move is usually that the present home is, or is likely to become, too big, too expensive to run or maintain, and eventually too difficult to manage.

It may have inconvenient stairs to climb, a lot of windows and floors to keep clean, a heating system that is not adequate or economical when you are at home all day.

Apart from the expense of a house and garden, and the worry about not having enough money for the necessary maintenance and repairs, when you get older you may feel exhausted and depressed by the physical struggle to keep a large old house cleaned, heated, and in good repair. Even a beloved garden may become a burden when everything grows faster than can be controlled.

On the other hand, maybe your accommodation now seems too small: a flat may have been quite adequate while you were at work, but when you are retired and spend much more time at home, a couple of rooms may not be enough.

But if you are thinking about moving to a larger place, consider carefully whether you have enough furniture and enough money and energy to start a new type of home.

Staying in the present home

If you decide not to move, it may be worth looking at your present home afresh, to see if the rooms could be more usefully arranged. The present arrangement of one bedroom, one dining room, one sitting room and one spare room could become two bedsitters, one study and a lounge with a large dining area.

Turning a spare bedroom into a workshop for d-i-y activities may be useful: the room will have electric sockets, possibly a water supply and will be a place to work in comfort without disrupting the rest of the household – and without having to clear up. Similarly, a small room where the sewing machine, and all that goes with it, can be left out permanently ready to use, and where a tailor's dummy will not be in anyone's way, may be a useful transformation from what used to be one of the children's bedrooms, now left intact for their occasional visits. If you transform all the spare rooms, however, try to make sure that you will still have room for visitors.

improving the home

Think about comfort and safety in the home and necessary repairs and possible improvements before you retire, while you have an income to cover any major expense. Now is the time for installing new equipment, and undertaking major decorations and maintenance.

If you have not had the wiring checked in the last ten years, have that done now by a competent electrician and, if necessary, have the house or flat rewired, and perhaps another circuit put in. If you are having any electrical work done, it might be a good ideal to have new sockets put in at a convenient place and height, where they are easy to reach.

Make sure that there is adequate lighting in every area of the house and especially on the stairs. If not, it may be possible to have two-way switches, so that you do not need to enter the house or cross the hallway in the dark.

Do not delay too long before dealing with house maintenance. The longer you wait before repairing a pipe or a leaking roof, the more expensive the repair will be.

A kitchen could be made more convenient, and safer, with adequate work surfaces. A new cooker is an expensive piece of equipment, so if yours has become inefficient, it may be worth replacing it now with a new, split-level one with a separate hob, which saves having to bend down to lift out hot dishes.

Shelves and cupboards are often too high or too low, so give some thought to reorganising what you keep where, to avoid having to use steps too often. A strong pair of steps, preferably with a platform and handrail is useful – get in the habit of using them instead of a stretch-and-balance act on the kitchen stool.

The bathroom may also need attention. Consider having a shower installed which uses less hot water than a bath and is therefore more economical.

Remember to review the security arrangements of your home. It may be worth contacting your local police station, by telephone or by going there in person, to make an appointment for the local crime prevention officer to come to your home and carry out a security survey inside and outside the house. He should be able to give you detailed advice on how to make your home more secure. The police do not charge for advice from the crime prevention officer.

Moving

If you decide that you need a different house, and will want to move, plan as far ahead as you can and do some thinking and researching.

when?

You may feel that you would like to live in your new home for a couple of years before you retire, so as to get to know the people and places as a 'working person' rather than a 'retired' one. However, if you decide to put off a move for, say, two years, you will have the opportunity to find out more about yourself and the sort of life you lead when retired, and therefore to have more idea of the sort of district and home that will suit you.

If you move immediately on retirement, you start your new life in new surroundings. But it may be more convenient to house-hunt and move when you have more free time for the actual business of putting your present house or flat on the market, finding and buying a new one, and the whole process of sorting out, getting rid of the accumulated junk of years, packing, and all the worry that goes with a move – even if it is only to a new home three streets away.

council tenants

Generally it is difficult for somebody who owns a house to get on the local authority list for a council tenancy, but if your house is large and would be suitable for conversion, you may be able to sell it to the council in exchange for a council flat or bungalow.

An existing council tenant who wants to give up a large family size house which has become too big may be able to get it exchanged for more suitable accommodation such as a bungalow or flat.

Some local authorities keep an exchange list of tenants who want to move into similar council accommodation to their present house or flat but in another area; or two tenants may be able to arrange an exchange independently. It is not easy to move into a different local authority, but most authorities keep lists of council tenants who wish to move to a neighbouring authority. It is more difficult to arrange a move to a local authority a hundred miles away, but an organisation called Locatex Bureau whose address is PO Box 1, March, Cambridgeshire, can match council tenants who wish to offer or exchange their tenancy with one in another part of the country. Locatex charge a small fee, usually around £7.

The Tenants Exchange Scheme has been introduced by the government to help public sector tenants in England and Wales who want to exchange homes with a tenant in another council's area. Details and a registration form, with notes on how to complete it, can be obtained from the Tenants Exchange Scheme, P.O. Box 170, London SW1P 3PX.

The National Mobility Scheme is a voluntary scheme agreed between most public housing authorities in the U.K. to help tenants move to a different area if they have a pressing need to move, such as an elderly relative who needs support. For more details, and a nomination for a move under the scheme, go to your own housing authority or housing association.

Some counties have mobility schemes operating within their own boundaries. The Greater London Council runs a seaside and country accommodation scheme for tenants over state retirement age. To qualify, you have to be a council tenant, fit and able to maintain a garden, and have to be nominated by your local authority.

A booklet *Wanting to Move?* (No. 12 in the Department of the Environment's series of housing booklets) is available from local councils and citizens advice bureaux. It gives advice to people wanting to rent (including privately) or buy in a new area.

some financial considerations

The points you should consider are:

☆ the size and value of your home now
☆ the size and value of the home you will need when you retire
☆ what you can buy elsewhere with the proceeds of selling the present home
☆ the income from investing any surplus lump sum, if what you get from selling is more than you need for buying
☆ the cost of moving
☆ the saving you could make in running costs by moving to a smaller house (rates, heating, maintenance); conversely, the increase if you move to a larger one
☆ the savings you may be able to make by living in a cheaper area (and vice versa).

If you think that it will make sense to move, get some idea of the value of your present home and also what you might have to pay for the kind of house or flat you want. Then make some estimate of the cost of moving (which may be up to 10 per cent or so of the value of your new house). You can then work out how much will be left for you to invest as a result of your move to give you more income, if you are worried that your income will be too low when you retire.

how often?

It is worth considering whether it is better to make only one move to a house or flat which will be suitable for the remainder of your life, or whether it is advisable to plan for two phases – the active and less active – and risk the unsettling effect of a second move at a later time when it may be less easy to adjust.

Difficult though it may be, try to anticipate your needs and attitudes ten, or even twenty, years from now. If there are two of you, consider also what kind of home would be suitable for your widow/widower living there alone.

Ideally, you will want a flat, bungalow or easily maintained house you like, in an area where you will feel safe, in a situation that will sustain you as you become older and less mobile, preferably near family or friends, with shops and transport facilities near, and which will not become too expensive to live in and maintain.

where?

Many people think of retiring to the country or to the seaside. However, at a seaside resort, property may cost more than it does where you now live (and food and services may be more expensive, too). Remember that it is very different living permanently in the middle of the country, or all the year round in a seaside resort, compared with spending a happy two-week holiday there in the height of summer. Apart from walks in the country and by the sea, will other activities be available to you?

assessing the location

It is a good idea to go and stay in the area you have in mind, wherever it may be, at different times of the year. Try and make an assessment of the area and what living there would entail, starting with the shopping.

○ How good is the shopping? Is most of what you need, or are likely to want, available in the locality? Are things more expensive than you have been used to?

You should try to do a genuine comparison of your 'shopping basket' cost for a week. That does not mean that you have to buy all the items, but try to go to the various local shops (not just chain supermarkets which probably charge the same wherever they are located), with paper and pencil and note down the prices. Do this for all that you would need to buy – not just groceries but also the prices of services such as shoe repairs, and dry cleaners, and cinemas, and afternoon tea in a local tea shop.

○ Is it possible to walk to shops, post office, library, a social centre? Are there facilities for you to carry on with a hobby, an interest, an evening course?
○ What is public transport like, would you have to depend on the car?
○ Does getting about locally mean having to go up and down a hill?

○ How easy would it be to visit friends and relatives, and for them to come to you?
○ Would you be happy, or at least content, to go on living in the area if your spouse or companion died, or would you want to move again?
○ What would happen in times of illness?
○ What is the situation about doctors or a health centre and ancillary services, such as chiropody?

If you are thinking of moving to an area that is popular with retired people, general practitioners are likely to have a high proportion of elderly persons on their lists, and may find it difficult to accept new patients.

In an area with a predominantly ageing population, there may be a strain on the welfare services and more people needing help than there are people able to give it. Try to find out, for instance, the length of waiting time for a chiropody appointment or an appointment at a hearing aid clinic.

Only if you decide you like the area in general and have checked that it is likely to be suitable for you, should you start looking for a particular flat or house.

necessary money

If you decide to move, one advantage of doing so straightaway is that there may be a lump sum from your pension to spend on a house (which may be vital if you have been living in rented accommodation and are an elderly first-time-buyer). A person who is approaching retirement age, or has passed it, may not be able to get a mortgage from a building society and would have to find some other lender. Also, an older borrower would probably have to provide additional security and may have to pay higher interest rates for a short-term loan.

home income scheme

Something to start thinking about in anticipation of being 70 or 75 years old is boosting your income with a home income scheme.

The schemes are available for freehold houses, and for leasehold property with a long lease of at least fifty years still to run.

You get a loan based on the security of your home; in other words, you raise a mortgage on it and use the money to buy an annuity, from an insurance company. While you live, you get the income from the annuity from which basic rate tax, and interest on the loan have been deducted; and when you die the mortgage is repaid out of your estate, possibly by the sale of the home.

With some schemes, you sell a part, or all, of your house to the company, so any increase in the value of the house then goes to the company and not to you or your estate.

When you apply for a scheme, an independent valuer will put a value on your home and the most you are likely to get by way of mortgage is 65 per cent of the market value.

If there are two people living in the house, for instance husband and wife, the annuity can be arranged so that it continues while one of them is still alive. If it is likely that you want to, or have to, sell your home, for example to move in with relatives, it is not a good idea to involve yourself in a home income plan because if you do move, you have to repay the loan. And remember that you cannot cancel an annuity and get your money back.

MOVING ABROAD

You may decide that you would like to live abroad after retirement, perhaps because you have visited a country on holiday and like the way of life there, or because you would like to escape to a warmer, sunnier climate. However, consider all the aspects and implications even more carefully than if you were intending to move to a new area in the UK.

The first decision is where to live, and then to discover, as far as possible, what it is like to live there. It might be worth spending a fair bit of time there before you retire, to explore the area to find out what living there really entails – as against being on holiday. Visit the area at different times of the year, not just during the peak on or off holiday seasons, when the atmosphere and the facilities may be atypical.

psychological aspects

Not speaking the language of a country would be a great barrier, so if you do not know it yet, make sure that you will be able to learn it. Even so, there is a risk of being isolated, or dependent on an expatriate group. You will probably see less of your family, certainly as far as casual visits are concerned (though they, and others, may want to spend their holidays there). If you go and visit them, the fares may be high.

You may think that eventually, when you are very old, you will prefer to be back in Britain and therefore buy a bungalow in Bognor. The tax implications of this are complex. Briefly, if you have accommodation available for your use in the UK, you are regarded as resident for any year in which you visit the UK, and ordinarily resident if you come here most years. The Inland Revenue leaflet IR 20 (Residents and Non-residents Liability to Tax in the UK) gives details.

Living abroad will involve a completely different lifestyle and therefore different attitude of mind; you should be aware of this before committing yourself to life in another country.

practical aspects

Remember, too, that services may be very different from those in the UK, such as no doorstep delivery of milk. It may be difficult, or very expensive, to obtain such everyday items as British newspapers. If you can, do speak to other British people living in the area and find out their views, and go shopping to see what is readily available, at what prices. Food may be cheap, health care and transport may be expensive, for example. Find out what the public transport system is like – expensive or cheap, reliable or unreliable, frequent or infrequent?

formal aspects

It is important to check pension arrangements in the country where you wish to live. Your state pension can be paid to you, free of UK taxes, in most parts of the world, but you would have to check with your local social security office whether subsequent increases in the pension can be received. Countries where increases are payable at present include all the EEC countries, Spain, Malta and Portugal; notable exceptions include Canada and Australia.

Health facilities are most important. See if a health service exists and whether you would be eligible to use it (and, if so, under what conditions). Local health insurance may be available; check whether your British private health insurance, if you have such a thing, covers residence in the country you want to live in. Try to find out what the standard of medical care is and what, if any, ancillary services there are for the elderly.

It is also vital to investigate local tax regulations; whether you need to become a registered resident of the country and what the conditions of doing so are; to make sure you understand your own legal position as a foreign resident. You may need to seek professional advice on these points; in the first place, contact the embassy of the country where you intend to live, to ask specific questions.

check list:

o health services, availability of drugs;
o resident's permit: how, when, for how long, restrictions, cost;
o work permit, giving (unofficial?) english lessons;
o tax abroad – income tax, dual taxation, local taxes (for residents/ foreigners);
o tax situation in UK while living abroad, earning, non-earning, short return visits to UK, double taxation relief arrangments;
o what happens when there is a change in exchange control regulations: effects on pension payments, effects on dividends, banking arrangements;
o professional advice abroad;
o social security and medical care agreements: see the DHSS leaflets for the relevant country, in the SA series, and (for EEC countries) SA. 29/Nov 80 *Your social security and pensions rights in the EC.*

FITNESS AND HEALTH

At any age, people feel better, look better and on the whole are generally healthier if they are not overweight and eat a sensible balanced diet, get adequate sleep and exercise.

A well-balanced mixed diet contains carbohydrates (bread, potatoes, rice), fats (margarine, milk, cheese), protein (meat, eggs, fish), vitamins and minerals in fresh fruit and vegetables. Wholemeal bread, coarse green vegetables, salads, unpeeled fruit and bran all help to provide fibre in the diet.

If you are used to eating lunch at your office or works canteen, make sure that after retirement you will continue having at least one proper meal each day when you have to provide it yourself. Try not to make up for missed meals by getting through packets of biscuits. Being at home all day you may be tempted to eat more: make sure that you keep an eye on your weight, following your retirement.

If you eat more than your energy expenditure requires, you get fat. Carrying too much weight makes people more liable to develop diabetes and diseases of the heart, and may aggravate arthritis.

The body requires at least three pints of liquid a day so that the kidneys can function effectively. There is no harm in beer or wine, in moderation, but too much alcohol can lead to health problems, quite apart from the other costs.

smoking

Even if you have been a smoker for many years, it is still worth stopping, today. By the time you are fifty or sixty, you are surely aware that smoking is bad for you.

A cigarette smoker runs a much greater risk of lung cancer than non-smokers do; cigarette smoking is not only associated with lung cancer, but also with coronary heart disease and chronic bronchitis.

Smoking can also reduce the appetite, blunt the sense of taste and smell, cause bad breath and indigestion, and alter the normal rhythm of the heart beat. Cigarette smoking, even in moderation, greatly reduces the chances of enjoying a healthy retirement.

There is no easy method of stopping smoking; most people who fail have decided only to 'try to give up smoking' rather than having made a firm decision to stop. Do not expect to succeed unless you have great willpower.

The Consumer Publication *Avoiding heart trouble* explains the risks associated with cigarette smoking, and offers advice on ways of giving up.

sleep

People differ in the amount of sleep they need. By and large, an adult's pattern of sleep is retained until the onset of old age. But there can be temporary upsets due to worry, pain or other physical disturbances.

Sleep is a habit which, if it is broken for whatever reason, can sometimes be difficult to re-establish. Because one of the causes of insomnia is worry and stress, the worry (justified or not) about the approach of retirement, and change of lifestyle associated with retirement, may make a previously sound sleeper develop less regular sleeping habits.

Insomnia is the persistent inability, real or imagined, to sleep. Anyone waking up very early feeling fresh and well has probably had enough sleep and is not suffering from real insomnia. However, people who repeatedly wake in the early hours and feel tired and depressed should consider getting help from their doctor.

People who take little exercise, or sit and doze in an armchair all the evening, should not expect to fall asleep the minute they go to bed and then to sleep all night. It might be a good idea to take a brisk walk before going to bed, as part of a regular bedtime routine. Some people find that a hot milky drink last thing at night will help them sleep, but they should not be misled into believing that special branded bedtime drinks have some particular sleep-giving quality; these have no advantage over any other non-stimulant hot drink. It is the routine that matters and can help people who have difficulty in falling asleep.

the bed

Also, make sure that your bed is comfortable. If you feel stiff when you wake in the morning, it may be for no other reason than that the bed is unsuitable. For good support, and a comfortable night's rest, the mattress should be firm and should not give by more than about two inches at any part. If your mattress is beginning to sag, now is the time to buy a new one; good mattresses are best on a firm solid base.

Although some people think that a so-called orthopaedic mattress would be a good investment for their retirement, there is no evidence that such a bed would do more for you than any other firm mattress on a good base.

aches

When you are standing or walking, be aware of your posture. Much back trouble can be prevented if the back and abdominal muscles are kept strong and in good tone and if you avoid stress on the spine, particularly in the region of the lower back. Be careful how you lift and carry heavy things. Your posture when sitting is important, too. A chair should support the small of your back and allow you to sit tall.

If you have persistent backache, or pain or stiffness in the joints, this may be due to arthritis. Consult your doctor.

Too many people attribute unpleasant symptoms to age when, in fact, they may have an illness which can be diagnosed and cured. If you feel unwell or notice that you now need to do things in a markedly different way, do not dismiss such symptoms as mere signs of approaching age.

seeing your doctor

Go and see your doctor about any symptoms that worry you, including

* ☆ pain in the chest (sudden or severe or persistent)
* ☆ continuous pain in the abdomen
* ☆ blood from any part of the body – in urine, in stools (making them look black) in sputum, in vomit
* ☆ localised weakness of an arm or leg
* ☆ breathlessness
* ☆ loss of weight
* ☆ hoarseness that persists
* ☆ a lump in the breast, in the groin, in the neck – anywhere in the body
* ☆ fainting
* ☆ persistent irritation of the skin, persistent itching, an ulcer
* ☆ unnatural tiredness
* ☆ frequent need to urinate
* ☆ marked change in bowel habits.

The doctor may be able to recognise a potentially serious disease – diabetes, high blood pressure, heart trouble, cancer – in its early stage, and carry out treatment at a time when it can be effective. He can send you for specialist examination if necessary. Many diseases come on insidiously and can be dealt with or avoided if action is taken in time.

And if there is nothing seriously the matter, the doctor can reassure you and advise you on what you should do to keep yourself in good health. You should never feel guilty about seeming to waste the doctor's time. There is no reason why you should think that you must put up with pain or discomfort, just because you are getting older. Middle age – or old age – is not an illness.

regular check-ups

Neglect in middle age can quite unnecessarily lead to loosing your teeth. Make a regular dental appointment every six months, even if your mouth seems healthy, but particularly if you show signs of bleeding, bad breath or loose teeth. You should go to a dentist who is prepared to take trouble with your gums and to give your teeth regular scaling. If you have dentures, get them checked every three years.

Most people need glasses for reading as they grow older. If you are finding it increasingly difficult to read or to see things near you, go and have your eyes tested. You do not need a doctor's referral: just make an appointment under the national health service with an ophthalmic optician or an ophthalmic medical practitioner. Regular eye examinations are important not only to get a prescription for reading glasses but also because diseases can be detected, such as glaucoma which can creep up on people without their being aware. If, in the course of a routine sight test, any suspicious signs are found, you will be referred to your general practitioner who may send you to a specialist in the hospital eye service.

private health insurance

There are private medical centres in London and some other cities, such as Nottingham and Manchester, where you can have a health screening test (for a fee of about £150; slightly reduced fee for members of the private health insurance responsible for the particular centre).

The older you are at the time of joining a private health insurance scheme, the higher the annual premium. The upper age limit for taking out private health insurance is generally 65 years but there are some special schemes for older people.

Exercise and sport

There will be more time for exercise and sports after retirement. If you have been in the habit of taking regular exercise, carry on – if you have not done anything physically active for many years and never thought of doing so, do so now. There is no need to feel that you are too old, or too flabby, or likely to make a fool of yourself. However, do not suddenly take up a new form of strenuous exercise and

○ do not take undue exercise when you are not feeling well or recovering from influenza or a bad cold
○ if you are not used to sports, start with only short periods of exercise and gradually and regularly increase the time and vigour
○ never ignore fatigue; take a rest when you are tired
○ avoid exercising to the point of severe breathlessness, pain or distress.

some suggestions

Walk, cycle, swim as much as possible, and keep going with any sport you have been doing. If you want to take up a suitable new one, the choice includes badminton, bowls, golf, table tennis, dancing (country and ballroom), keep-fit. A form of exercise particularly suitable for people as they grow older is a chinese form of keep-fit called Tai Chi Chuan which is a pattern of movements designed to keep all the limbs flexible. It is a kind of gentle, contemplative dancing. Classes are held at adult education centres, and other places, and once you have learned the movements, you can carry on by yourself.

The Sports Council has a series of '50+' leaflets with suggestions for out-and-about activities (such as hiking, rambling, orienteering, bird watching); for 'sports centre activities', including their likely costs and the equipment needed; on 'lending a hand', with suggestions for participating in the activities of a local sports club. These leaflets should be available at your local library.

When you are retired, you will be in a position to use sports facilities during the less crowded parts of the week, such as public tennis courts at three o'clock on a tuesday – the time when you used to be at your desk – and the swimming pool at ten in the morning.

Swimming is not only very healthy, at any age, but has the advantage that you do not have to rely on finding a partner or a team. On the other hand, there is an advantage in taking up, or continuing, a sport that allows (or even forces) you to meet others.

A good first contact is your local sports centre or the recreation department of the local authority. The regional office of the Sports Council (headquarters at 16 Upper Woburn Place, London WC1H 0QP, telephone 01-388 1277) will also be able to help with suggestions and local addresses.

learning to enjoy leisure

Even a person who has been looking foward to retirement as an opportunity to expand his or her interests and develop a new lifestyle will need a period of adjustment after perhaps 45 years of regular employment. When suddenly there are no deadlines to be met, no regular journeys to get to work, no need to leave the home at a specific time every day, and the whole day is yours, you may wonder what to do with all this freedom.

Being free does not mean being idle. Leisure can be used for doing things out of interest rather than for money, doing what you have always wanted to do – including pottering around, gossiping, reading with your feet up and relaxing.

Perhaps there will be a different slant to leisure. If, during your working life, you led a very sociable life, it may have been a relief to get away on your own. In retirement, however, you may feel the need for company of like-minded people and therefore decide to join an association, club or group – which is a good thing for someone who has no longer the usual everyday contact with fellow workers.

There are groups and associations for most leisure activities, and being one of a group also imposes some discipline: if the weather is bad, you are more likely to go out for a game of golf if it has been arranged with others, than force yourself to go out for a walk alone. When free time is unlimited, you may need to exert more self-discipline than you would have imagined, in order to do even the things you most enjoy.

classes

While working, many people start courses or evening classes – but fall by the wayside. Many of these classes may be on offer during the day, under the auspices of the local education authority. The Workers' Education Association (Temple House, 9 Upper Berkeley Street, London W1H 8BY) also offers a varied selection of day time and evening classes. There is no reason why a retired person should not continue to go to evening classes, nightschool, adult education courses.

The University of the Third Age promotes self-help educational activities – run, taught and attended by retired people. For information about local groups, contact the executive secretary, Mrs. D. Norton, 6 Parkside Gardens, London SW19 5EY.

trying new activities

Some colleges and community centres provide facilities for people to experiment with several hobbies or activities before committing themselves to buying equipment and paying course fees. In some centres, the skilled members teach each other various crafts (and thus course fees are kept to a minimum).

Here is a short list of hobbies you may not have thought of, but may want to give a try:

brass rubbing, caligraphy, car maintenance, cooking, copper/pewter work, corndolly craft, dressmaking, embroidery, jewellery making, lampshade making, leathercraft, macramé, marquetry, painting, pottery, sketching, soft furnishing, weaving, woodwork.

Despite cuts in education budgets, if there is a demand for a particular type of class, most authorities will do their best to try to meet it. Classes may include: astronomy, comparative religions, creative writing, genealogy, languages, musical appreciation, philosophy, public speaking, yoga. The cost of classes varies from area to area, but there may be some reduction for retired people.

It may be possible to join an amateur dramatic or an amateur operatic society, not necessarily as the leading tenor or even to take a walk-on part, but helping behind the scenes, to make props, to sew costumes, to be the 'resident electrician', to sell programmes on the night.

People usually take up a hobby for their own pleasure but may find that in retirement they have more time to share it with others. The model railway enthusiast will easily find many enthusiastic youngsters to share his interest, and there is always an audience for anyone who has studied local history and local architecture.

Remember that it is more important to enjoy the activity than to achieve perfection. If you are hesitant about speaking in front of people, take a public speaking course. However, be realistic. Not many people are going to change drastically in late middle age. While inside every shy retiring mouse there may be an extrovert lion trying to get out, if that has not happened by the age of 58, it is unlikely to happen after a public speaking course at 62 or 68. Or if you have 'always wanted to write novels' but never found the time to put pen to paper, it is unlikely that you will turn into a Jane Austen at 61.

being prepared through pre-retirement courses

Many companies think that it is not their responsibility to prepare their staff for retirement. But in fairness to some employers who do, employees are often reluctant to attend pre-retirement courses, perhaps because they do not want to think about, or plan for, their own retirement (maybe they think that, like accidents, it is something that happens to other people).

If your firm does not provide a pre-retirement course, bring the matter to the attention of the personnel department, the staff association, your trade union branch. The Pre Retirement Association, 19 Undine Street, London SW17 8PP (telephone: 01-767 3225) has published a booklet (price £3.50) *Colleges and centres providing pre-retirement courses* which lists them in alphabetical order from Avon to Yorkshire in England, and includes Scotland, Wales and N. Ireland. The courses are mainly held at colleges of further education; most are run by the local education authority, some by private firms. Some are residential.

Preparation for retirement is obviously concerned with hard practical matters – finance, housing, health. It should also help to prepare you for more leisure, and deal with family and emotional relationships and how the change in routine will affect you in your new life.

DOMESTIC ADJUSTMENTS

Where the husband's and the wife's relative ages are such that he retires while the wife is still working full-time, the situation can produce special stresses. A man may be lonely and feel neglected while his wife is still working, especially if his own retirement is unwelcome. He may therefore need considerable emotional support. On a strictly practical level, it may be worth sitting down together and deciding who does what in the new regime. The man might have to learn to contribute more to the practical running of the home, now that he spends more time there. There may even be a small lesson there for a man who could not understand what the wife did all day long . . .! However, it is unlikely that a man who has never ironed his own shirts (let along anyone else's), will suddenly want to do so now, or find great fulfilment in doing such tasks. But vacuuming, dusting and polishing, doing the shopping, are jobs that do not require a long apprenticeship.

A man may have been holding down a responsible job for years, but not know how to cope with finding himself alone in the house with a shopping list and set of instructions for the family meal. Start preparing him gently, now. Some men are excellent cooks. He should be encouraged to watch the tv cookery course, or attend a cookery course at the local tech, or nightschool or adult education centre. Some run special courses just for men.

There may be a sudden realisation that everybody else seems to be pursuing their own goals, including the children who may now be offering advice to their father in his new role. All these situations of role-reversal call for tact and understanding on everybody's part, and it may take time to adjust.

Message to wife at retirement stage: can you mend a fuse, fill in a tax form, mow the lawn and mend the lawnmower, do the decorating, turn off the mains water? Get him to teach you now – he may not be around forever. And vice versa.

women

Some of the effects of retirement are different for women than men, whether they are themselves retiring, or living with a man who is about to retire.

Where the man has retired and the wife does not go out to work, it can mean less freedom for her. A non-working wife who is used to her own routine may find it difficult to adjust to having someone around all the time. She has her own friends, her hobbies, her own way of life. Perhaps she is used to a snack lunch (or none at all) and now is expected to produce a cooked meal every midday.

The need for understanding and adaptation within the family is vital. Men may find it difficult to adjust to being around the house all day, too. In this situation, both parties need to use tact and understanding to adjust gradually to their new situation.

In retirement, most couples will be seeing more of each other than ever before in their married life, so what may have been a minor irritation, because they were not spending so much time together, might become a source of real friction. You may decide to grin-and-bear it; or, by putting words to a problem, it may turn out to be something trivial, after all. If it unleashes thirty years' bottled-up resentment, that, too, may be a good thing if it helps to clear the air a little.

It is not always appreciated that a woman's retirement from work affects her just as a man's does his. Women who started, or resumed, work after having a family or looking after a relative can, particularly, miss the companionship and interests outside the home, and the mental stimulation, which a job provides. A man may assume that housework will provide his wife with something to do, to fill the gap after retirement, but forgets that one of the reasons why many woman go out to work is to prevent their housework expanding into a full-time job. She may not relish a return to a life dominated by household chores.

single people

Anyone living alone may particularly miss the companionship of colleagues at work, and there may be a feeling of isolation to cope with, as well as adjustment to a life no longer centred round work. But the actual pattern of domestic life may not be all that much disrupted and, for a gregarious person, the change may not be very dramatic.

If you are single or widowed and faced with living alone in your retirement, you may need to make a special effort to get involved with your neighbours and invite friends or acquaintances home – not necessarily for a meal, but perhaps for coffee or, now that afternoons are free, for tea.

Offer your services as a babysitter and you may become the most sought-after person in the street. Perhaps do some shopping for someone who is housebound. Try to keep in contact with all age groups and, particularly, avoid falling into the trap of separating yourself from young people, even if you are mutually suspicious. If you have any expertise to offer or experience to share with young people, explore ways of becoming involved in helping them. But do not approach them on a senior-to-junior level: that is a recipe for disaster.

Consider inviting a student to live with you, as a paying, or non-paying guest. Contact the accommodation officer at your nearest college or university or teaching hospital. Tell him or her the type of student you would prefer: male or female, young or mature, for example, so that you will get somebody who would not be disruptive to your way of life. Many young people and mature students are serious and conscientious, some are lonely, especially overseas students. With a bit of give-and-take, the advantages (including the financial contribution) could outweigh the disadvantages, and may in fact work out extremely well for all concerned. If not, you can always opt out of it next term.

Putting affairs in order

Some people have their affairs in order all the time, but for those who have not, the run-up to retirement or perhaps immediately after having retired, when you have more time on your hands, is a good opportunity to sit down and take stock. For people who are planning to move house, there may be a need to sort things out, to throw out old papers and clobber and be forced to get themselves well and truly organised.

Both partners should know where important documents are kept, insurance policy for house, car, life insurance, deeds to property, share certificates, and so on. A person living alone who, in an emergency, would be dependent on neighbours, should have placed in some obvious position the telephone number and address of a close friend or relative who could be contacted.

have you made a will?

Making a will does not mean that you are going to die one minute earlier; not making a will may well mean that your possessions, after death, will go to someone to whom in life you would not have given them. You may think that it will all go to your wife/husband anyway, but he/she may die before you. Whether it will all automatically go to the spouse depends on how much the 'all' is, and whether there are any surviving children, or possibly surviving parents. The Consumer Publication *Wills and probate* sets out clearly what happens to the possessions of a person who dies intestate (that is, without having made a will) and describes what is involved in making a will.

considering CTT

One important matter to bear in mind when making a will is that capital transfer tax has to be paid on most gifts, and in this context a legacy or bequest counts as a gift. Moreover, the capital transfer tax payable on death is at a higher rate than on lifetime gifts. However, there are some exemptions from CTT, the most relevant of them, in this context, is that each year a person can give away £3,000 without tax; that on death, no CTT is payable on £60,000 of what is left; and that gifts (in life or on death) between husband and wife are free of CTT. This is an advantage if you plan to leave it all to your wife/ husband. But bear in mind that tax will then have to be paid when he or she dies. So it is worth considering, all other things being equal, to make a will that uses up the £60,000 tax-free allowance in favour of, say, children.

appointing executors

It is usual to appoint executors, in a will. An executor is the person whose responsibility it will be to see that the wishes expressed in the will are carried out. To do so, the executor of a will has to obtain a grant of probate (which involves a certain amount of paperwork and calculations), pay the CTT (not out of his own pocket, but he has to make the arrangements for the payment), pay off the debts of the person who has died, and make sure everything is perfectly in order, before distributing the property to the people who are to benefit from the wishes expressed in the will (the beneficiaries). It is therefore a responsible, time-consuming job, even when everything is quite straightforward. Often two people are appointed to be executors, to share the burden. It is a good idea to appoint one or more of the main beneficiaries as executors, who have a stake in seeing that the administration is carried out as smoothly as possible.

Although it is not binding on the person who is named in a will to act as executor when the time comes, it is best to ask first, before making the appointment, so as to give the person a chance to say 'no' and to let somebody else be appointed.

As one grows older, it is inevitable that certain friends and relatives will die. There is no need to avoid discussion of the subject. For instance, if someone you care for feels strongly about, say, cremation or formal rites, it is right that you should know – and vice versa.

power of attorney

Many people at retirement age have elderly relatives who may be finding it increasingly difficult to look after their own affairs. It may be advisable to get a power of attorney for them.

A power of attorney is a simple document which gives one person authority to act on behalf of another. It can be drawn up by a solicitor, or you can use one of the forms published by the Solicitors' Law Stationery Society, Oyez House, 237 Long Lane, London SE1 4PU (form Conveyancing 36 or Conveyancing 37), available from Oyez shops. Or you can do it yourself. All that a general power of attorney needs to say is that a person (X) appoints another (Y) as his or her attorney in accordance with section 10 of the Powers of Attorney Act 1971.

The document must be dated, sealed (have a little disc representing a seal stuck on it), and signed in the presence of a witness. A 50p Inland Revenue stamp has to be affixed. Not all I.R. offices are stamp offices. You can find out where your nearest one is from the information section, Controller of Stamps Office, Southwest Wing Bush House, Strand, London WC2B 4QB (tel. 01-438 7039).

It need not necessarily be used immediately, perhaps never. The elderly relatives should continue to be in charge of their own affairs as they were before. But in the event of, perhaps, a stroke or something which prevents them from writing or dealing with official papers or, for instance, the bank, the power of attorney is there to be used.

WORKING AFTER RETIREMENT

A person who has retired may want to find work for financial or for personal reasons, such as getting out of the house, companionship, involvement.

If you are past retirement age, remember the 'earnings rule': you lose 5p of basic pension for every 10p you earn over £65 a week up to £69, and 5p for every 5p (that is, pound for pound) earned over £69. And anything you earn may effect the amount of tax you have to pay. So you may find that to make it worthwhile, you would have to earn a high salary or fee, perhaps higher than you can demand. Your earnings count for the week in which they are earned, even if you do not receive them until later. If you do not know in advance how much you will earn, your pension may be reduced in line with an estimate of what your earnings might be, and will then be adjusted when the final amount is known. It is always worth checking beforehand to see if and how your pension will be affected.

occasional jobs, freelance work

Even in today's economic climate there are employers who may be glad of someone who is willing to work for, say, two or three hours a day, or one day a week, perhaps saturdays (cinema queue-marshall, checking weekly holiday makers in and out of hired accommodation, doing workshop repairs for a store) earning just within the limit. There are seasonal jobs for a retired accountant to prepare small firms' books, for an ex-civil servant to advise on form-filling; someone to man the office when all the workmen (boss included) are out on jobs; a handyman to do an accumulation of repairs in, or decorate the outside of, a house, or do odd-job gardening.

Employers know how much a retired person can earn without his or her pension being affected. The remuneration can often be tailored to fit the pensioner's free limits, but beware of being exploited. It may be tempting to accept cash-in-hand payment, but it is probably better to insist on the rate for the job and be ready to pay tax on it.

In today's economy, it may be difficult to obtain even part-time employment on a reasonable salary, but it is quite possible that voluntary or 'expenses-only' work can be found – possibly more than one job. Voluntary jobs, although not offering a salary or pay, may cover travelling expenses (and give you the opportunity to travel – even if it is only to the other end of town), and expenses such as post and telephone calls.

Telephone calls, even if they are strictly for business purposes, mean that you have to be in communication with outsiders: a defence against the isolation that some people fear in retirement.

voluntary work

Many people do voluntary work in a limited way without really considering it as voluntary work – that is, by helping neighbours in the community. After retirement, with more leisure, it is possible to do so in a somewhat more organised way. In some respects, voluntary work can offer some of the bonuses that employment gave you: company, outside involvement, a sense of personal value and an up-to-date reference, which should be particularly useful if you decide to try a part-time return to work in the future.

There are many voluntary organisations, and in every sphere there is always demand for volunteers, not only for the large national organisations, but in local ones – for example, local housing organisations, local hospital, local Oxfam shop. The Employment Fellowship runs activity centres to enable people to use their skills and maintain contact with other people. They always need volunteers. For details of your nearest centre, contact the Employment Fellowship at Drayton House, Gordon Street, London WC1H 0BE (telephone: 01-387 1828).

Many councils of social services run voluntary workers' bureaux which are designed along the lines of an employment exchange.

In paid employment, people usually have some idea of the hours they will work, the type of work they would like to do and the money they would like to earn. Some of the same considerations apply to voluntary work, so be prepared to ask about them at any voluntary workers' bureau. Make sure that if you are going to do voluntary work you will not be out of pocket: if you are offering your services free, do not hesitate to ask if your expenses will be covered.

enjoy it

Many of us have to spend our working life doing jobs we are not particularly keen on because we need the money, but this is not a consideration with voluntary work in retirement. Every voluntary organisation has a wide variety of jobs on offer, and skills needed. Think what skills you have to offer (and want to offer) before deciding to contact any organisation.

Do something which you are going to enjoy because there is little point in doing voluntary work unless you are going to get some satisfaction from it. If the smell of hospitals makes you feel upset or uneasy, there is no point in going to do voluntary work in a hospital. If you do not care for children, then working with them would be a mistake. If you are put on 'fund raising' and find this is uncongenial, ask for an alternative job – say office work or something within the scope of your capabilities which you will be happy and comfortable doing.

If you have been dissatisfied with the job you have been doing for the last ten or twenty or more years, and been eagerly awaiting the opportunity of retirement, think carefully before going back to doing the same thing – but without the pay.

An important consideration before offering yourself for voluntary work is how much time you really want to give. When you have quite a lot of free time, you may want to be very generous with it. But voluntary work snowballs: if you have not had any experience of it, a good idea is to offer a couple of hours to begin with, and then do more if you enjoy it and find that it is not going to encroach too much on your freedom. Sometimes volunteers deal with people who become very dependent, so that it is difficult to resist demands – until the 'two hours' develops into four or more.

On the other hand, we all like to feel that we are needed and voluntary work can give a great deal of satisfaction.

help exchanges

Exchanging help for help is not a new concept and good neighbours have been doing it since time immemorial.

Often people who do not fall into any particular category of great need would like a little help from time to time – with the garden, income tax returns, redecorating, shortening the sleeves of a jacket, seeing what is wrong with the car – and yet are unable to pay much (or anything) for it because they are retired and living on a limited income. It would only take a few retired people living in the same area to set up a bank of skills, offering one hour of a skill in exchange for an hour of any other skill. Self-help groups need not be restricted to retired people. An exchange of skill on a time basis could extend to every member in a community and all age groups.

CONCESSIONS

some things you can do cheaply

Once you reach state retirement age (65 or 60) you will qualify for a number of concessions and benefits. For some, you need proof of age, and perhaps proof that you are a resident of the area; for others, you have to be able to produce your pension book. Someone having the pension paid directly into the bank, should ask the local social security office for form BR 464, so that a card giving proof of retirement age can be sent from the Department of Health and Social Security; this card can be used instead of a pension book to obtain concessions.

Travel

Most local bus companies, both those run by the local authority and privately run ones, let senior citizens travel either free or at reduced rates. There may be restrictions, such as no concessionary travel during certain hours; or extra bonuses, such as allowing a companion to travel free or at reduced rates at weekends.

Find out what the situation is in your area, from the local bus company; a bus conductor may be a good first contact.

trains

The British Rail senior citizen railcard costs £12 for one year. The card entitles you to ordinary single and return tickets and 'awayday' tickets at half price. You can take four children aged between 5 and 14 with you, for £1 each. But the reduction does not apply to weekend or monthly return tickets, or to any special offer. There is also a 50 per cent discount on Sealink ships to the Channel Islands, Irish ports and the Isle of Man; for travel on inter-city sleeper services you have to pay the full sleeper supplement but only the half-price fare.

You can also buy a £7 card which entitles you to day-return tickets at half price. With this, too, you can take up to four children with you under the same conditions as for the £12 card. They do not have to be your own grandchildren or other relatives, so this is an opportunity to take a neighbour's or a friend's children on an outing.

A senior citizen railcard also entitles you to reduced travel on the London underground.

There are certain restrictions about trains on which the concessionary fares do not apply. British Rail have leaflets which give up-to-date information.

air travel

A reduction of 30 per cent on the full normal round-trip fare for any flights within the UK is available on British Airways. The return journey must not be until six days after the outward flight.

foreign rail travel

Many of the European railway companies offer reductions to their own senior citizens, some extend these to foreign travellers. For example, in France, men over the age of 62 and women over the age of 60 can buy a *carte vermeil* for £5, and get a 50 per cent reduction on French railways, but there are some restrictions on the times of travel during which the *carte vermeil* is valid.

A 50 per cent discount is given in Austria on railways and post buses to men over 65 and women over 60 who obtain a special identity card (price 140 Schilling); in Germany, a railways senior citizen pass costs the approximate equivalent of £25 and gives a 50 per cent reduction.

A British Rail senior citizen railcard entitles you to buy, for £5, a Rail Europe Senior card which gives savings on the cost of travel from the UK to 17 continental countries and on journeys within those countries, namely

☆ up to 50 per cent reduction on railways in Belgium, Finland, France, Greece, Holland, Luxembourg, Norway, Portugal, Spain, Sweden, Switzerland

☆ up to 30 per cent in Austria, Denmark, Hungary, Italy, West Germany, Yugoslavia

☆ up to 30 per cent on sea crossings by Sealink and by Hoverspeed, when the crossing is part of a rail/sea through journey.

The main restriction on the use of a Rail Europe Senior card is on travel which starts in one of the foreign countries during parts of the weekend. But if you start your journey in this country and travel through to your destination without any stopover, the fares reductions do apply even for weekend travel.

holidays

In retirement, life might seem one long holiday, but even so it is important to think of getting away from home, if only for the odd day, for the stimulation of seeing and doing different things and having a complete break from the usual routine.

Some tour operators specialise in holidays for older people, which usually means over 55 years of age. The Greater London Association for Pre Retirement has compiled an information sheet (No. 7 holidays) which gives details; your local Pre Retirement Association may produce a similar information leaflet.

Most of these holidays are for out of season periods.

leisure activities

Some theatres offer reductions for matinees or some mid-week evening performances, usually one ticket per person – so if you go with someone below retirement age you may sit side-by-side for different prices.

Local authority concessions will vary from area to area, but might include reduced entrance to swimming baths at off-peak times of day; waived fines on overdue library books; museums, stately homes, art galleries and exhibitions that normally charge an entrance fee may waive or reduce it. Some clubs and associations offer membership at a reduced fee or allow non-members above retirement age to buy tickets (such as the National Film Theatre in London). Many ordinary cinemas offer seats at half-price for their afternoon performances. The admission fee for some sport events may be reduced.

Even private businesses, such as dry cleaners and hairdressers, may offer reductions.

All this varies from place to place, so you will have to keep your eyes open for notices and, if in doubt, ask if there is an OAP reduction.

NHS concessions

When you reach the official state retirement age, prescriptions are free. Just tick the box on the back of the prescription form and fill in the details in the space provided.

making ends meet

You may think that you are too well-off to qualify for any help, but if you find it difficult to meet ends meet, make sure you know what you are entitled to, by checking with your local social security office or the social services department at your town hall.

supplementary pension

A person over the state retirement age, who is not in paid full-time work, and whose resources are less than his or her requirements (both according to official definitions), may qualify for a supplementary pension in addition to any state retirement pension. It is a non-contributary pension, that is, not dependent in any way on the number of NI contributions a person has made. To be eligible, the gross income (less various allowable expenses) must be less than the set figure, which depends on whether you are a single person or a married couple, and on some other factors. The supplementary pension is not taxable.

Leaflet SB1, available from local social security offices or post offices, gives details and a claim form.

You will have to give particulars of all your income, and other detailed information, in a personal interview with someone from the social security office. You can choose to have this interview in your own home rather than at the social security office.

Anyone in receipt of a supplementary pension is automatically entitled to other benefits. For instance, they may qualify for help with heating costs if they are in poor health, live in poor housing, have central heating or are aged 70 or over.

If you have a low income or claim supplementary pension, you may be able to claim help with fares to and from hospital. Get leaflet H11 for further information.

Someone getting a supplementary pension will be repaid the charge for national health service spectacles. Anyone with an income only just above supplementary benefit level can also claim repayment. An optician can give you the claim form (F.1) to send in.

Dental treatment is free if you are receiving supplementary pension (make sure you tell your dentist, and ask him for form F1D); you may also qualify for free treatment or help with charges if your income is low.

useful organisations

In all situations where you may need explanations about official documents, or need help and advice generally on any official or legal or administrative matter, or want to ask questions about pensions, the local citizens advice bureau might be able to help.

If necessary, you can find out the address of your nearest citizens advice bureau by getting in touch with the registry department of NACAB, 110 Drury Lane, London WC2B 5FW (telephone: 01-836 9226).

The Pre Retirement Association of Great Britain and Northern Ireland, 19 Undine Street, London SW17 8PP is mainly concerned with encouraging pre-retirement education. The majority of members are companies, but private individuals can join; generally they join their local, affiliated, organisation. There are some thirty local Pre Retirement Associations (in some localities known as Pre Retirement Council or Retirement Association, or Pre Retirement Committee). They include GLAP (Greater London Association for Pre Retirement) and PRAGMA (Pre Retirement Association of Greater Manchester) and may be county-wide or concentrate on a single locality. You can find out the address of your nearest Pre Retirement organisation from the PRA headquarters in London.

Choice, the monthly magazine of the Pre Retirement Association, available from newsagents at 75p, gives advice on a variety of topics, including health, housing and finance.

INVESTMENTS

Decisions about investment for retirement have to be made not just at the time you retire but in the years leading up to retirement.

When you have worked out how much income you will have when you retire, you may realise that it may be wise to try and spend less money now and invest it, so that you can have more later, when you have retired.

Saving can be done on a regular basis in an organised scheme, or in an ad hoc manner, putting aside odds and ends as you get them. But do not just put the money aside, invest it.

Even if you are not familiar with investing money, you may find that now you have to make decisions about it.

planning ten years or so before retirement

If you have ten or more years to go to retirement, you could consider a scheme linked to life insurance, assuming your health is good. Such schemes include unit-linked life insurance, or a with-profits endowment policy (which is a somewhat steadier way of saving).

Do not start either of these savings schemes unless you can keep up the payments. Remember that the money will be tied up for ten years (or the period you agreed to save for). It is not wise to enter into a long-term financial commitment shortly before retirement.

If you have between ten and five years before you retire, some ways of saving are:

○ unit trust savings schemes – a feasible way of saving, but can be risky because you could lose money instead of making a capital gain
○ index-linked National Savings Certificates – guaranteed to keep pace with inflation
○ index-linked gilts – for a lump sum only
○ National Savings-Certificates – safe but they give an unexciting return, except for higher-rate taxpayers.

planning four or five years before retirement

One way of saving which may be particularly good in the last few years before retirement is by making additional voluntary contributions. It depends on your own particular pension scheme how good an investment this will be for you – for instance, whether the employer matches your contributions, or not.

Other ways of saving suitable for this comparatively short period until you retire are

○ index-linked National Savings Certificates
○ building society subscription shares.

planning a year or so before retirement

Your choice of saving methods is now more limited. If it is a wise decision to make additional voluntary contributions, you should still be able to do that. You could still consider index-linked National Savings Certificates or building society subscription shares.

investing a lump sum

As you come up to retirement, you should be planning how you will use or invest any lump sums you may get. These could come from several sources:

☆ many pension schemes pay out, or give you the choice of, a tax-free lump sum in place of part of your pension;

☆ you may have got a lump sum from moving to a cheaper house; also from the sale of your car;

☆ you may have accumulated a lump sum from saving and investments you have made over the last few years. But if the investment you made in previous years was money invested in an insurance company fund (for example, a property fund or managed fund), you should be careful about when you cash it in, because it could affect your tax bill when you have retired. Also, it may not be the best time to realise such a lump sum because of the state of the market.

You may decide to 'invest' part of a lump sum on enriching your retirement, for example, getting a really good workshop, or a hi-fi, or installing central heating, or going on the holiday you could never before afford.

To someone retiring with a lump sum, it may be the first large sum of money he or she has ever had. That is exciting, and also alarming, so do not be tempted simply to put it all into the building society, without considering all the options.

You can, of course, ask for advice from investment advisers such as a bank manager, insurance broker, accountant and the like. But remember that advisers get paid commission by all sorts of organisations – building societies, insurance companies, unit trusts, for example. So the advice may not be quite as unbiased as you think. In general, you should try to find out about investments and make your own decisions: it is your money, so you should care more than anyone else.

how investments differ

Investments can differ in several ways: the return, they give; how they keep their value; when you can get your money back; the tax position.

○ *The return:* what you get back from an investment can come in two different forms. Firstly, you might get an income paid out to you in interest or dividends. Secondly, with some investments, you expect (or hope) that the value of the money you invested will rise and give you a capital gain.

In practice, these two different forms of return can overlap. In some cases, you can add the income to the money you have already invested so that the value of your investment will rise. You can also cash bits of any capital gain, to give yourself an income.

○ *The value of the money you invest:* can stay the same in ££££ (but it may only seem to do so because inflation will be eroding its real value); an example is a building society investment. Or the value of the money you have invested can go up and down (this is riskier because you could lose money; on the other hand, you hope you will make a capital gain and help to protect your investments against inflation); an example is a unit trust.

Sticking to safer investments, such as building societies, means that you may stand less chance of keeping up with inflation than with, say, an investment in a unit trust.

○ **When you can get your money back:** with some investments you cannot get your money back until the end of an agreed period; an example is an income bond, which is an investment offered by a life insurance company usually lasting somewhere between four to ten years.

With some other investments, such as a building society or bank 'fixed notice of withdrawal' account, you agree to give a period of notice (for example one week, or three months) and can get your money out at the end of the period of notice. But in many cases you can get the money back at once, although you may lose interest.

Some investments have no time restrictions but the value rises and falls, and may be low when you want to cash the investment and it may be prudent to wait for a suitable moment to get your money back.

○ *Tax:* different levels and ways of taxing can make one investment very good for a higher-rate taxpayer, unattractive for a low taxpayer, and so on. The most suitable investments for higher-rate taxpayers are usually tax-free ones where the return is mainly a capital gain rather than income.

Non-taxpayers will find it advantageous to choose investments which pay an income without basic rate tax being deducted. Building society investments are usually not attractive to non-taxpayers because they cannot claim back the tax that has been deducted from building society interest.

a fund for emergencies

If possible, everybody should have some money put aside for an unexpected emergency. There may be expenses caused by sudden illness, major repairs to the home or to the car, and so on. For this type of need, you should have money invested in a way that makes it easy to get at and where there is not too much risk that there will be a fall in its value just when you have to cash it. The size of the emergency fund depends on each person's needs and particular circumstances, but most people should think in terms of around £500 to £1,000.

Suitable investments for an emergency fund include:

○ bank deposit account – where you can in practice cash your investment at once, although you may lose some interest
○ building society ordinary account – but there may be a limit on how much you can cash at once
○ National Savings ordinary account – you can cash only £100 at once at Savings Bank post offices (or £250 with a 'regular customer' account at a post office designated by you) and rates of interest are unattractive on sums of less than £500.

a fund for a definite purpose

When you retire, you may make definite plans about what you want to do in, say, six months' time, or in a year, or in two years. For example, you may want to get a new car or go on an expensive holiday. For this purpose, too, you will need a type of investment where you can be confident that the value of the investment will not fall and that you can get the money when it is needed. If you can definitely leave your money for one or two years, it widens the choice. Suitable investments include:

o National Savings Bank investment account
o fixed notice of withdrawal accounts and term accounts which are offered by banks, building societies and companies which are licensed deposit-takers
o deposit accounts and ordinary share accounts offered by banks and building societies
o index-linked National Savings Certificates which guarantee to keep pace with inflation.

funds for boosting your income

Investments which will give you an income now or in a short while include:

o an annuity
o investments in building societies, banks and companies which are licensed deposit takers; these pay out interest
o National Savings Bank investment accounts and National Savings income bonds; the income bonds pay out a monthly income (but the minimum investment is £2,000)
o income bonds which are offered by insurance companies for a fixed period – four to seven years, say
o local authority investments
o index-linked National Savings certificates (if you cash some certificates).

For longer-term investments, consider investing in shares, unit trusts or single-premium investment bonds.

funds for boosting your income later

Inflation erodes the value of a fixed income or of one which depends on interest alone. Therefore, you should consider investing for less income when you first retire, so that you can increase it in later years and so try to mitigate the effect of inflation. One way of trying to achieve this would be to invest part of your lump sum for growth, rather than income, to try to get an increase in its value. Then in perhaps five or seven years, if you find that you need to boost your income, you could cash this investment and reinvest it to give you more income. Suitable investments for this include:

o unit trusts which aim for capital growth (these will pay out very low incomes)
o shares
o single-premium investment bonds such as property bonds, managed bonds, equity bonds
o index-linked investments such as index-linked British Government stock (gilts) in which the value of your money is linked in some way to the retail price index.

Details of investments

Here is a brief outline of some types of investments (in alphabetical order, not in order of priority).

annuities

You can buy an annuity for a lump sum from a life insurance company and it gives you a guaranteed income until you die.

For example, in return for £10,000, invested in April 1983, a 75-year old man who paid tax at the basic rate could have got an after-tax income of about £1,800 a year for life.

There are several different sorts of annuities. Probably the commonest is an annuity that pays you a level income, at regular intervals, starting six months after you bought it. It is usually not worth considering buying one until you are about 70, although you can get annuities from a younger age. The younger you are, the lower the income you will receive. A woman is likely to get a somewhat lower income than a man of the same age, because on average women live longer.

You may get more, or less, income as a result of opting for one of these variations:

○ You can get an ***increasing income annuity,*** instead of a level income one. Choosing this variation means that you will start off with a lower income. For example, assuming an annuity which increases your income by 5 per cent a year, it will take some seven or eight years for an increasing annuity to pay the same income as a level one. And, at present rates of inflation, much longer (perhaps 16 years), for you to receive the same total buying power.

○ You can get an annuity which carries on paying until both the person buying the annuity and someone else (usually a wife or husband) are dead. These are called ***joint life and survivor annuities.*** They pay less income for the lump sum.

○ A variation of a joint life and survivor annuity is one where less income is paid after the first person dies – perhaps half or two-thirds of the amount paid while both are alive.

○ Payments can be made more or less frequently than twice a year; for instance, once a month. More frequent payments mean a slightly lower income in total.

○ Instead of getting an income starting straightaway, you can get a ***deferred annuity*** where the income starts some time after you have made the payment – for example in five years' time. Therefore what you get paid will be considerably more.

○ You can get an annuity where payment is **guaranteed** for a number of years (usually five) even if you die – in which the case the money goes to your estate. Generally this means that the income is reduced by about 3 per cent.

Although annuity rates vary frequently, you continue receiving the rate that applied when you bought your annuity. So, the fixed rate you get may mean that you do well, or badly, depending on what happens to interest rates after you bought the annuity.

You can find the latest rates in magazines such as *Savings Market, Money Management* or *Policy Market* (obtainable from libraries). Check with the company first that the rate you have seen is still being offered.

tax:

Part of the income from an annuity is a return of some of your lump sum and part is interest which has been earned on it. Only the interest part of what you get back is taxed and is normally paid after deduction of basic rate tax: it is treated as investment income. With an annuity which you have to buy as part of a personal pension plan, the whole payment is taxed as earned income.

drawbacks:

An annuity is basically a gamble. With most types, if you die (even the day after you make the payment), your heirs cannot get any money back. Interest rates may rise or fall after you buy, but your income is fixed. Also, the value of a level income annuity can be eaten away by inflation.

advantage:

It is guaranteed until you die.

bank investments

The high-street banks offer several investments:

o *A bank deposit account* is a suitable place for odds and ends and for keeping your emergency fund, particularly for a non-taxpayer. For a taxpayer, a building society generally pays better interest. The minimum you can invest is generally very low; it may be as little as £1. In theory, with most deposit accounts you have to give seven days' notice if you want to get your money out. In practice, the bank will pay out on the spot, but may deduct seven days' interest. Interest is worked out every day and is usually added to your account twice a year.

With scottish banks, the interest is worked out on the minimum amount you have in the account during each month – so if you withdraw your money, there will be no interest at all for the month during which you withdraw it.

○ A *fixed term account* offers either a fixed rate of interest (as at the date of your deposit) or varying rates of interest. The periods for which you can invest vary from a few weeks to several years, but are fixed at the outset and you cannot withdraw the money earlier. The minimum sum of money you can invest varies from several hundreds of pounds to many thousands of pounds.

○ A *'fixed notice of withdrawal' account* offers a rate of interest which varies with interest rates in general. When you invest your money, you agree to give a fixed period of notice before you can cash it. The period of notice varies from scheme to scheme – it may be one month, or three or six months. The minimum amount you can invest also varies – from £1,000 to £5,000, say.

tax:

The interest on any bank investment is taxable but is paid without deduction of tax (which makes it particularly suitable for a non-taxpayer).

drawbacks:

The income from bank investments is generally variable and has little protection against inflation. With a fixed-term account, you cannot withdraw any money until the end of the period for which you agreed to invest.

advantage:

A bank deposit account is safe where the bank is 'recognised' by the Bank of England. There is a Deposit Protection Fund which will pay 75 per cent of the first £10,000 you have invested if the bank should fail. Make sure you invest your money only with a 'recognised' bank.

British Government stocks

The government issues British Government stocks (also called gilt-edged securities) as a way of borrowing, and these stocks pay interest to the holder, usually twice a year. The interest is fixed (except with the variable rate stock). Conventional British Government stocks could suit two different sorts of people:

☆ those who want a regular income
☆ those who want to invest for a specific time period because the maturing dates are fixed (this means that at a certain moment you get back your lump sum).

British Government stocks are bought and sold on the stock exchange, and prices can go up and down. Roughly speaking, the price of stocks fall if interest rates in general rise, and vice versa.

The return from a British Government stock is made up of two parts:

○ interest payments (always the same, except with variable rate stock)
○ capital gain or loss, depending on the price you buy and sell at (or get at the end of the life of the stock when it is redeemed at face value).

When you buy British Government stock, you know when it will come to an end, for instance not until 2016, or in 1994, or as early as 1986. If you want to get your money back before then, you can sell the stock, but there is no guarantee of the price.

Ways of buying and selling British Government stocks are through a stockbroker or through the National Savings Stock Register. If you do not know a stockbroker, ask your bank to help. You can get more details about, and an application form for, the National Savings Stock Register from your local post office. When there is a new issue of British Government stock, you can buy direct by filling in a coupon cut from newspapers such as *The Times* or *Financial Times* or *Daily Telegraph*.

tax:

Interest is taxable, but is paid without deduction of tax if the stock is bought through the National Savings Stock Register. If you buy through a stockbroker, or newspaper coupon, interest is normally paid after deduction of basic rate tax. If you hold the stocks for a year or more, any capital gain you make on selling is free of capital gains tax; but if there is any loss, it cannot be offset against other capital gains.

drawback:

There is no protection against inflation.

advantages:

British Government stocks are suitable if you want a fixed income for a known period. If interest rates go down generally, to below the interest rate of your government stock, you could do very well both because of continuing to get a comparatively high income and, if you want to sell, the price of the stock would be high.

building society investments

Different building societies offer slightly different investment facilities and the names they give to the different accounts may vary – the interest rates may also vary slightly.

○ *Ordinary share* (and *deposit*) *accounts* are suitable as a home for your emergency fund and for saving odds and ends of money. The minimum investment is low – usually £1. Most building societies' rules gives them the right to insist on a month's notice for withdrawal but, in practice, you can normally get £250 or so in cash, or up to £5,000 by cheque on the spot. (Deposit accounts pay a slightly lower rate of interest than ordinary share accounts because they are deemed to be slightly safer.)

The Building Societies' Association runs a protection scheme. If your money is in a deposit account and the society goes bust you will get back all your money. For share accounts, the amount guaranteed depends on whether the society contributes to the scheme or not. If it does, you are guaranteed to get back 90 per cent. If your society does not contribute, you are guaranteed 75 per cent. So, before you invest, ask if the society is a contributing member of the protection scheme.

Another feature which should make for extra safety is the society having trustee status. To qualify for this, a society has to meet certain financial requirements laid down by the government.

○ A *subscription share account* is suitable for saving a regular sum of money – the minimum is often £1 a month.

○ *Fixed notice of withdrawal* or *penalty shares* limit you to getting your money out after an agreed period of notice – such as one week, one month, three or six months. But, with most, you can cash your money immediately and lose interest for one week (or one month or three or six months).

With some accounts you do not have a choice of agreed period of notice, but have to pay a penalty for cashing on the spot. There may be a minimum you can invest, such as £500 to £2,000. The rate of interest paid will be higher than the rate on an ordinary share account – perhaps ½ per cent to 1½ per cent more.

○ *Term shares* have all sorts of variations. With some term shares, you have to leave your money for the period you agreed to invest for and really cannot withdraw any; but with most, you can cash all or part of your investment if you give, for example, three months' notice – and you have three months' interest deducted. With a few term shares, once you have come to the end of the agreed period, you can leave your money invested in the account and get a guaranteed increase in the interest rate as well as easier withdrawal terms.

Another variation is that the longer you leave your money invested (up to a maximum of five years, say) the higher the interest rate paid for each extra year. The minimum investment for term shares is usually £500 to £1000. The rate of interest paid will always be higher than the rate for ordinary shares – perhaps 1 per cent more.

○ *Monthly income accounts* are offered by some building societies; such an account pays out a monthly income. Or, more usually, you can have your income from a term share or a fixed notice of withdrawal or penalty share paid monthly. To get this, you may have to make a bigger investment, perhaps over £1,000.

With all building society accounts, the interest will usually vary with interest rates in general. On most accounts, interest is added twice a year (once a year for subscription shares).

tax:

There is no basic rate tax to pay on the interest you get from a building society investment. But if you are a non-taxpayer, you cannot claim back the deducted tax. If you are a higher-rate taxpayer, or pay the investment income surcharge, you will have to pay extra tax on the grossed-up income.

drawbacks:

Little protection against inflation; not usually suitable for non-taxpayers.

advantages:

Building society investments safe; a building society ordinary share account is suitable for an emergency fund.

finance company deposits
(and other licensed deposit-taking institutions)

There are three main types of account for deposits:

○ *A fixed term account* paying a fixed rate of interest. You cannot normally get your money back until the end of the term for which you agreed to invest. The minimum investment is in the range of £1,000 to £5,000.

○ A *fixed notice of withdrawal account* which means that you can get your money out if you give the agreed period of notice, such as one, three, or six months. The rate of interest paid on these accounts will vary. The minimum investment is generally around £100, but ranges from £1 to £5,000. Interest is normally added to the account or can be paid out twice a year.

○ So-called *money funds* which allow you to get at your money at once, or in a few days. The rate of interest goes up and down and the minimum investment is high – £2,500 or £5,000, say.

Licensed deposit-taking institutions are licensed by the Bank of England provided they meet certain requirements. There is a Deposit

Protection Fund, which will pay out 75 per cent of the first £10,000 you have invested if the deposit-taker were to fail. Make sure you invest your money only with a licensed deposit-taker. It is not worth losing the protection of UK laws for the extra ££'s you may get by investing in one which is not licensed (it would have to be based outside the UK but this could mean the Isle of Man or Jersey).

tax:

The interest paid on these accounts is taxable but is normally paid without deduction of tax.

drawbacks:

No protection against inflation. With fixed term accounts, you cannot withdraw the money until the end of the period for which you agreed to invest.

advantage:

Suitable for non-taxpayers.

income bonds

This sort of investment is offered by life insurance companies and pays out income at a fixed rate for an agreed period. At the end of the period, but not usually before, you get your money back. The period may be four to ten years. The minimum investment you can make varies from company to company but is generally £1,000.

tax:

The tax treatment depends on how the bond works. Check carefully with the company, before investing, that the proceeds from the income bond will not affect your age allowance (the special tax allowance for people who are aged 64 or over at the start of the tax year).

drawbacks:

Income bonds provide no protection from inflation. This investment may be unsuitable for people getting age allowance.

advantage:

They give a fixed income for an agreed period.

index-linked British Government stocks

If you hold the stock from when it is issued until it matures, it is guaranteed to keep pace with inflation. At redemption, it is worth the face value of the stock, increased in line with inflation over the lifetime of the stock. Currently there are nine stocks each with a different life. (ending for example, in 1988, 1996, 2006, 2011 and up to 2016) The stocks pay a small income (interest rate of either 2 or 2½ per cent) which is also increased in line with inflation. You can buy two of these stocks, the ones ending in 1988 and in 2011, through the National Savings Stock Register, the rest through a stockbroker or via your bank.

After the stock is issued, it can be bought and sold on the stock market, so the prices fluctuate. The return you will get depends on the price you buy and sell at.

tax:

The interest is taxable but is paid without deduction of tax if the stock is bought through the National Savings Stock Register. If you buy through a stockbroker, interest is normally paid after deduction of basic rate tax. If you hold the stocks for a year or more, any capital gain you make on selling is free of tax but any losses cannot be offset against capital gains.

drawbacks:

Income from index-linked British Government stocks is small and the price of the stock can go up and down.

advantage:

Depending on the price you buy and sell at, these stocks give some protection against inflation.

index-linked National Savings certificates

This is an investment offered by the government which guarantees that the value of your investment will keep pace with inflation as measured by the retail price index.

The certificates do not pay an income as such, but their value increases cumulatively in line with inflation. You have to compare the expected rate of inflation with the expected after-tax return on other investments to help you decide whether they are worthwhile.

If you hold them for five years, you get an extra bonus of 4 per cent. However, if the certificates are cashed within a year of investing in them, you get back only what you invested without any increase. You can cash units after one year and get back their value, increased in line with any increase in the retail price index.

The minimum investment per person is £10, the maximum £10,000; the investments are in units of £10.

If you want to use the certificate to receive an income, you can cash some units.

tax:

The return is tax-free.

drawback:

The return depends on inflation.

advantages:

Index-linked National Savings certificates are a safe investment which guarantees to protect your money against inflation; the return is tax-free.

local authority investments

There are three sorts of investments:

○ *Local authority loans* last for a fixed term, between 1 and 7 years. The local authority pays interest on the loan – this interest is usually fixed. Once you have invested the money, you cannot usually get it back until the end of the agreed period. The minimum investment is generally between £250 and £1,000.

○ *Local authority stock* when it is first issued, can be bought direct from the local authority. After that, it can be bought or sold on the stock exchange, so the price of the stock goes up and down and if you sell you get the going price – which may be more or less than you invested. If you hold the stock until it matures, you will know what return you are going to get – namely the face value. Interest, usually fixed, is paid on the stocks. Because of the costs of buying and selling, the minimum sensible amount to invest would be £700 or so.

○ *Yearling bonds* work in a similar way to local authority stock but they usually last a short time, most commonly one year.

You can get information on which local authority is currently offering a good return by telephoning the CIPFA's loan bureau (Chartered Institute of Public Finance and Accountancy) between 3.30pm and 5pm, mondays to fridays (01-828 7855).

tax:

Interest is taxable and normally paid after deduction of basic rate tax; unlike British Government stock, local authority stock does not benefit from the capital gains tax exemption, so there is a possibility of tax on capital gains.

drawback:

Local authority investments provide no protection against inflation.

advantage:

They provide a fixed income for a definite period.

National Savings investments

There are several sorts of investments:

o On *National Savings certificates* (25th issue in March 1983) you get agreed interest added (but the interest cannot be withdrawn unless you cash the certificates). You get the full advertised return (at present 7.5 per cent) only if you hold the certificates until the end of the agreed period – 5 years with the 25th issue. You can cash before this, but the return is lower – for example, 6 per cent for the first year.

o A *National Savings ordinary account* (used to be the old post office savings bank) gives a low rate of return (3 per cent on sums less than £500). For sums over £500, left for a complete calendar year, interest rate is (currently) 6 per cent. Interest is added on 31 December, for the preceding calendar year.

You can cash your money at any time, but only up to £250 on the spot, at most post offices. It can take a week or so to get the balance.

o A *National Savings investment account* pays a higher rate of interest than the ordinary one (at present 10½ per cent, added once a year), but you have to give one month's notice to withdraw money.

National Savings deposit bonds interest is currently 11½ per cent. Each bond costs £500 but you can invest more money in multiples of £50. You have to give three months written notice to withdraw the money, but lose interest if you withdraw during the first year. You must leave a minimum of £500 invested.

o *National Savings income bonds* pay interest monthly (currently at 11 per cent, but the rate can change). Each bond costs £1,000; the minimum number you can buy is 2 and the maximum 200 and you must leave a minimum of £2,000 invested. If you want to get back some of your money, you have to cash one complete bond (or several) and you have to give three or six months' notice. If you cash within the first year, you get no interest at all on money withdrawn at three months' notice and only half the interest on money withdrawn at six months' notice.

After the first year, there is no reduction in interest on money withdrawn at six months' notice; but with only three months' notice you get no interest during the notice period on the money to be withdrawn.

tax:

The return on National Savings certificates, and the first £70 of interest on ordinary accounts, is tax-free. All other interest is taxable, but paid without deduction of tax.

drawbacks:

There are restrictions and possibly financial losses if you want to cash a National Savings investment.

advantages:

They are safe; the income bonds have the advantage of giving a monthly income.

shares

You invest your money in one or more (preferably several) companies. The return you get is made up of two parts:

○ income in the form of dividends paid by the company
○ capital gain when you sell (or loss, depending on whether the share price rises or falls).

Be careful about cashing your investment: do not necessarily do it on a pre-ordained date – for example, the day you retire – because this may be a time when share prices are low. You should be prepared to leave your money invested for a long time, because of this fluctuation in price. Ideally, get the advice of a stockbroker about what to buy and when to sell (which should be free because you will be paying his commission when you sell). If you want to keep an eye on how your shares stand, look them up in the financial pages of the newspapers.

To reduce the risk connected with investing in shares, you should try to invest in several companies, perhaps eight or ten, in different types of holding. Because of the cost of buying and selling shares, it is not generally worthwhile to invest less than about £6,000 to £8,000.

You buy and sell shares on the stock exchange, through a stockbroker or via your bank or other agent; there is a scale of commission which starts at 1.65 per cent of the value of each transaction up to £7,000. You may be charged more for small sums.

tax:

Income from the shares is paid tax-deducted: there is no more basic rate tax to pay, but if you are a higher-rate taxpayer you will have to pay more tax on dividends you get. If you are a non-taxpayer, you can claim back the tax that has been deducted. Any capital gain, when selling shares, is liable to capital gains tax.

drawbacks:

Investing in shares is chancy: you are taking the risk that you will lose money in the hope of getting a greater return. Treat them as having to be a long-term investment, but be willing to sell at the right time, either to realise capital, or to reinvest for higher income.

advantage:

Shares give some chance of protecting yourself against the effects of inflation, depending on when you buy and sell.

single premium investment bonds

You invest your money with a life insurance company and the value of your investment is linked to one of several funds the company runs, such as property bonds, commercial property, managed bonds (a mixture of property and shares, and fixed-interest investments), equity bonds (shares), British Government stocks, and so on.

With many companies you can, at a low cost, switch your bond from one fund to another.

Technically it has a life insurance element but should not be considered as such if you need real life insurance cover for the benefit of your dependants.

The bonds do not normally pay an income as such, but you can get an income by arranging to cash part of your investment either from time to time or on a regular basis. As long as you do not cash in more than the equivalent of 5 per cent of your original investment, what you draw out is tax-free at the time.

You will get a capital gain from the bond if the value of the fund (and your bond) rises. However, the value of your investment will depend on when you buy and sell.

The minimum investment you can make varies – usually £1,000 but it can be as little as £200. If you want to be able to cash bits to get an income, the minimum investment may be higher – £1,000 or more.

tax:

If you choose to, you can cash up to 5 per cent of your original investment each year without paying tax at the time, though you may have to when you finally cash the bond. If you pay tax at higher rates, or have to pay the investment income surcharge, when you cash the bond there may be tax to pay on any gain.

drawbacks:

With single premium investment bonds there is some risk of losing money in the hope of making a gain; treat as a long-term investment. There is an initial charge and an annual management charge.

advantages:

Depending on when you buy and sell, this investment gives some sort of prospect of protecting yourself against inflation. It is also a convenient way of investing in property, if that appeals to you.

unit trusts

This is a way of investing in the shares of UK and foreign companies and, with some trusts, in British Governments stocks. If you have less than about £6,000 to £8,000 to invest, this way of doing so is less risky than investing directly in shares. A unit trust is invested in many companies so, if one company does badly, you lose only some of your money.

You can choose to invest in a unit trust which specialises in investing in another country or area of the world, for example USA, the Far East and so on. Also, you can choose between funds which aim to give a high income and those which concentrate on growth. Your return will be made up of

○ income paid in the form of 'distributions', made up from dividends from the shares the unit trust invests in; you can usually choose to have the income reinvested in more units rather than paid out.
○ capital gain (or loss depending on whether the prices of the units you buy rise or fall). The success of your investment depends on when you buy and sell.

The minimum you can invest is generally in the £250 to £500 range. Once you have made an investment in a trust, you can add smaller sums later.

tax:

Income from a unit trust is paid tax-deducted: there is no more basic rate tax to pay on the income (called distribution) you get. But if you are a higher-rate taxpayer, you will have to pay more tax. Non-tax-payers can claim back the tax that has been deducted. Any capital gain is liable to capital gains tax.

drawbacks:

There is a risk that you will lose money with unit trusts in the hope of making a capital gain. Be prepared to treat them as a long-term investment. There is an initial charge, and an annual management charge.

advantages:

Depending on when you buy and sell, this investment gives some prospect of protecting yourself against inflation. It is also a convenient way of investing abroad if that appeals to you.

unit-linked savings plans

These are similar to single-premium investment bonds, except that you invest by paying regular small sums usually monthly or quarterly over a ten-year (or longer) period. You can cash the plan at any time, but may get back less than you invested for two reasons:

o the price of the units goes up and down as share prices, property prices, and so on, rise and fall
o the insurance company makes annual charges which can be high, particularly in the first two years of the plan.

The minimum you can invest varies; it is normally between £5 and £25, but much higher if you want a plan with lower charges.

tax:

The government subsidises the premiums (currently to 15 per cent) because the savings plans are linked to life insurance. The lump sum return from the plan is tax-free so long as you pay tax at no more than the basic rate, and tax-free to anyone (irrespective of their tax rate) who keeps the policy going for at least ten years, or three-quarters of its agreed term, whichever is less.

If you cash within the first four years and make a gain, you will forfeit some of the subsidy. The fund will pay tax on capital gains. This may be reflected in the price you buy and sell at, or the company may pass on the charge to you when you cash your units.

drawbacks:

Charges in the first few years of a unit-linked savings plan can be heavy; treat as a long-term (10 years) investment. Prices of the units go up and down, so be careful when you cash in.

advantage:

They give some chance of protection against inflation.

with-profits endowment policies

You invest your money with an insurance company which invests it in a fund. The value of your investment will increase, with bonuses added periodically to the policy; the bonuses depend on investment profits. In any event, you will get a guaranteed amount at the end of the agreed period (or when you die, if that is sooner), but your return should be higher than that. Most insurance companies also pay a terminal bonus when the policy matures. This one-off bonus, announced at the end of the policy term, is quite unpredictable and therefore does not necessarily imply that the policy is better than one without a terminal bonus.

The minimum you can invest is usually £5 a month – for how long has to be agreed before you start saving; it is usually 10 years or more.

You can cash your investment at any time, but what you get back is at the discretion of the insurance company and may be little, or nothing, in the first couple of years.

tax:

Because the saving is linked to life insurance, the government subsidises the premiums (currently the taxman pays 15 per cent to the company and you get the benefit of this). The lump sum return from the policy is tax-free if you pay tax at no more than the basic rate, and it is tax-free irrespective of your own tax rate if the policy is kept going for at least ten years (or three-quarters of its agreed term, whichever is less).

drawbacks:

Cashing in a with-profits endowment policy during the first few years means a financial loss, so treat as a long term investment (for the period you agree to invest for, which is at least ten years).

advantages:

They give a steady, if unexciting, return and a lump sum if you die – but if you want life assurance to make provisions for your dependants, this is not likely to be the right type of policy.

Tax

The two main types of tax which affect investments are income tax and capital gains tax.

income tax

Some types of investment income are tax-free, but most types are taxable. Taxable investment income is added to your earned income and taxed in the normal way – at basic and higher rates. If your total investment income is more than a certain amount (£7,100 in the 1983/84 tax year), you have to pay investment income surcharge of 15 per cent on the excess, in addition to basic or any higher-rate tax.

If you are a higher-rate taxpayer, consider putting your money in tax-free investments, or try to increase the value of your money, getting a capital gain rather than income.

age allowance

Tax rules for the elderly are much the same as for everyone else – except that anyone who is 64 or over (or whose wife is) at the start of the tax year can claim a special age allowance instead of the ordinary personal allowance.

This special age allowance is bigger than the ordinary personal one: for the 1983/84 tax year it is £2,360 for a single person while the ordinary personal allowance is £1,785, and the age allowance for a married couple is £3,755 (as against £2,795).

However, once your 'total income' exceeds a certain amount (£7,600 in the 1983/84 tax year), the special age allowance is reduced rather sharply. It is reduced by two-thirds of the amount by which your total income exceeds the £7,600 limit (until you get only the ordinary allowance).

'Total income' is normally your gross income less:

- interest payments you make which qualify for tax relief
- personal pension payments you make (unlikely to apply to a person at retirement age)

– the gross amount of any covenanted payments and enforceable maintenance payments you make.

So, if your income is so high that each extra £ of taxable income loses you some age allowance, investments where the return is tax-free (for example, National Savings certificates) may give you a higher after-tax return than, say, a National Savings investment account. You should also be careful about cashing in all or part of a life insurance policy on which you will make a taxable gain. Although there is no basic rate tax to pay on such a gain, it will be included in your 'total income', and so could reduce your age allowance.

If you pay tax at higher rates and you cash in a life insurance policy or make it paid-up in its first 10 years (or within the first three-quarters of its term if that is shorter) you will make a taxable gain.

claiming tax back

With many types of investments, such as local authority loans, the income is paid after tax at the basic rate has been deducted. Similarly, with dividends from shares and most unit trust distributions, what you get will have no more basic rate tax to be paid and will be accompanied by a tax credit. Your gross (before-tax) income is taken to be the dividend (or distribution) plus the tax credit.

If your tax bill comes to less than the total of tax deducted plus tax credits received, you will have paid too much tax, and should therefore claim a tax rebate.

You may be sent a special *Tax claim form R40* instead of the normal kind of tax return. If you have to claim tax back regularly, but are not sent form R40, ask your tax office for it. You should fill in this form and send it back to your tax office with your tax vouchers (which give details of tax deducted and tax credits). You do not need to wait until the end of the tax year to do this – claim as soon as you have received all your relevant investment income for the tax year (April to April). The taxman will work out how much tax you are owed and send you a rebate. Arrangements can be made for repayments of tax by instalments during the year – ask your tax office for details.

If you claim only occasionally, write to your tax office, giving details of why you are claiming and how much, if you know.

capital gains tax

You make a capital gain or loss whenever you sell or get rid of something. Anything you own can be included: a house, unit trusts, expensive jewellery.

Some gains are normally tax-free, for example:

* gains on your own home
* gains on British Government stock held for a year or more
* prizes won by premium bonds
* gains on National Savings certificates
* gains on personal belongings, antiques, jewellery, and other moveable objects, provided the value of each object when you sell it is £3,000 or less.

how much capital gains tax?

There is no tax to pay on the first £5,300 a year of net taxable gains. You deduct your losses from your gains to find your figure of net taxable gains for the year. The rate of tax on net taxable gains over £5,300 is at 30 per cent.

From March 1982 or from twelve months after you first became the owner (whichever is later), the value of anything likely to be liable to capital gains tax will be indexed (linked to the retail price index), so you are less likely to pay tax on 'gains' which are simply the result of inflation.

How investments are taxed

investment	liable for income tax?	has basic rate income tax already been deducted from income?	any higher rate income tax to pay? (or the investment income surcharge)	liable for capital gains tax?
annuities	yes – on the part which is interest	yes, normally	yes	no
bank investments	yes	no	yes	no
British Government stocks	yes	yes – normally if bought through stockbroker; not if bought through National Savings Stock Register	yes	not if held for more than a year
building society investments	yes	not as such but no more basic rate tax to pay – cannot claim tax back if non-taxpayer	yes	no
deposits with licenced deposit takers	yes	depends on company	yes	no
income bonds	yes	depends on way bond works – ask company	depends on way bond works – ask company	no
local authority investments	yes	yes	yes	yes – stocks, yearlings
National Savings bank	yes – but not first £70 of interest on ordinary account	no	yes	no
National Savings certificates	no	no	no	no
National Savings Deposit and Savings Income Bonds	yes	no	yes	no
shares	yes	not as such but no more basic rate tax to pay	yes	yes
single-premium investment bonds	yes – may have to pay higher rate tax when finally cashing the bond	no – but no basic rate tax to pay (fund pays tax)	yes – when you finally cash bond	no – but fund pays tax on gain
unit trusts	yes	not as such but no more basic rate tax to pay	yes	yes

Some relevant *Which?* reports

burglar alarms	Han	81	Feb	life insurance:			
cars: reliability	Mot	82	Jan	advisers	Wch	84	Feb
central heating:				local authorities:			
fuels/boilers	Wch	81	Jul	social services	Mon	82	Dec
dental charges	Wch	82	Jul	National Savings			
dental health	Wch	80	Apr	interest	Wch	84	Feb
doctors: complaints	Wch	79	Feb	NHS: waiting lists	Wch	80	Sep
doctors: GPs	Wch	83	Jul	opticians' prices	Wch	83	Mar
doctors: registering	Wch	79	Apr		Wch	84	Feb
draught excluders	Han	81	Aug	pensions: state	Wch	83	Oct
electrical wiring	Wch	84	Feb	rate rebates	Mon	81	Dec
food: heart disease	Wch	82	Jan	rates, paying less	Wch	83	Mar
food: nutritional					Wch	84	Mar
value	Wch	76	Jan	redundancy	Wch	83	Jun
fuel bill payment				rent rebates	Wch	83	Apr
schemes	Wch	84	Feb	safety in the			
gardening, easier	Wch	83	Mar	home	Wch	79	Mar
health insurance,				social security			
medical bills	Mon	82	Jun	benefits	Mon	82	Dec
heating and the				supplementary			
elderly	Wch	79	Jan	benefits advice	Wch	84	Feb
home improvements:				vitamin pills	Wch	84	Jan
grants and loans	Wch	82	May	window locks	Wch	83	May
	Wch	83	Feb				
	Wch	84	Feb				
home income schemes	Wch	83	Oct	Mon	*Money Which?*		
housing associations	Mon	78	Dec	Wch	*Which?*		
investments: easy				Mot	*Motoring Which?*		
withdrawal	Wch	83	Jul	Han	*Handyman Which?*		
jobs: legal rights	Mon	81	Jun				

There are many other reports in *Which?* that may be relevant and useful to you. Reports on domestic equipment such as washing machines, refrigerators, cookers, appear frequently; a car buying guide is published every October and every March the *Tax saving guide* is available to *Which?* subscribers.

Index

Earning money at home

for anyone who wants or needs to make some money at home, this book sets out what this entails in the way of organising domestic life, keeping accounts, taking out insurance, coping with tax, costing, dealing with customers, getting supplies. It also includes suggestions for different activities, including some that do not require previous experience.

Wills and probate

stresses the importance of making a will, explains how to prepare one, sign it and have it witnessed. It gives examples of different types of wills showing consideration for the effects of capital transfer tax. The section about probate deals in detail with the administration of an estate, without a solicitor, and illustrates how to deal with any problems that might arise.

Where to live after retirement

tackles the difficult subject of a suitable place to live in old age. The book offers practical advice on the decision whether to move or to stay put and adapt the present home. It weighs up the pros and cons of the alternatives open to an older person, and the financial aspects involved, considers sheltered housing and granny flats, the problems of living in someone else's home, and residential homes.

Which? way to buy, sell and move house

covers all the stages involved in moving to another home, including advice on mortgages, the costs of moving, what sort of property to buy, conveyancing, completing, selling the present home and planning the move.

Dealing with household emergencies

gives basic facts about what to do when a sudden emergency occurs, such as blocked drains and pipes, electrical failure, fire. It also includes some first aid advice and how to make an insurance claim after an accident or damage.

Securing your home

gives advice on how to minimise the risk of a burglary; locks, burglar alarms and general safety precautions are all covered. It also explains what to do and not to do if a burglar has broken in to your home (or car), and how to claim on your insurance.

The legal side of buying a house

covers the procedure for buying an owner-occupied house with a registered title in England or Wales (not Scotland) and describes the part played by the solicitors, the building society, the estate agent, surveyor, Land Registry, insurance company, local authority. It takes you step by step through a typical house purchase so that, in many cases, you can do your own conveyancing, without a solicitor. It also deals with the legal side of selling.

Raising the money to buy your home

tells you where to go for the money, how much you can borrow, and the types of mortgages available. It takes you through the steps of applying for a loan, and deals with what happens if you have difficulty in keeping up with the payments, or want to pay off your mortgage.

Getting a new job

deals with job hunting, how to apply, what to do to get an interview and how to make sure it goes well. It discusses the points to consider when being offered a job. The book also discusses redundancy, explains your rights and how redundancy payment is calculated.

Cutting your cost of living

suggests ways of spending less money without changing your standard of living. The book includes ideas on how to reduce your bills for food, heating, household appliances and holidays. It gives warnings about false economies and guidance on how to take advantage of what is available free.

Living through middle age

faces up to the changes that this stage of life may bring, whether inevitable (in skin, hair, eyes, teeth) or avoidable, such as being overweight, smoking or drinking too much. It discusses the symptoms and treatment of specific disorders that are fairly common in men and women over 45, discusses psychological difficulties, the possible need for sexual adjustment. Throughout, practical advice is given on problems that may arise.

What to do when someone dies

provides a clear practical guide to all tha may need to be done, including getting a doctor's certificate, registering a death and obtaining the various death certificates. Differences between burial and cremation procedure are explained. The book also explains the various national insurance benefits that may be claimed.

Avoiding heart trouble

identifies the factors which can contribute to heart trouble and describes how the various risk factors—cigarette smoking, raised blood pressure, stress—interact with dietary factors and overweight. It explains the more serious signs and symptoms of heart trouble, and where possible, tells you what can be done about them.

Avoiding back trouble

advises on ways of avoiding back trouble, and for those who suffer from backache already, offers guidance on how to ease it, how to live with it and how to avoid becoming a chronic sufferer. It deals with causes of back trouble, specialist examination and treatment and gives hints on general care of the back when sitting, standing, lifting, carrying, doing housework, gardening, driving.

The Which? Book of saving and investing

This big hardback book is a detailed guide to saving and investment opportunities. It includes advice on investing in particular circumstances, such as on early retirement. Subjects covered include pensions, lump sum or income, saving for a home, living on a fixed income, how to secure a significant addition to it, spare time earnings: how they can qualify you for extra income on top of your pension, while at the same time reducing the tax bill on these earnings.

The Which? Book of Money

Another of the big hardback books which covers the whole field of family finance. Topics include income tax, redundancy, mortgages, insurance, rates and grants, retirement planning, owning a car, private health insurance, passing your money on, life insurance, social security benefits and tax.

The Which? Book of Do-It-Yourself

tells you how to take advantage of the clever devices and labour-saving materials on the d-i-y market to save £££s on home repairs and improvements by carrying out the work yourself. All the different types of work are explained clearly and with illustrations where possible. Advice on how to make your home more secure is also included.

In preparation   **The Which? Book of Insurance**

Other Consumer Publications include:
Central heating
Living with stress
Making the most of your freezer
On getting divorced
Pregnancy month by month
Starting your own business
The newborn baby
Which? way to slim

Consumer Publications are available from
Consumers' Association, Castlemead, Gascoyne Way,
Hertford, SG14 1LH, and from booksellers.